PRAISE FOR STAND FI

"Leaving a legacy that speaks to your core values, values that are the heart of your beliefs and passion for business excellence, called Bob to write this book. Years of experience, and hours in prayer seeking God's wisdom have provided Bob with insights that allow the reader to journey with him and explore the possibilities that come from holding to God's teaching, walking in His protection and blessing. Written by a businessman for business men and women, *Stand Firm with God's Power in Business* is more than a book, it's the instruction manual most business schools have forgotten."

—*Gary Armstrong, CEO, General Air Services and Supply, Inc.*

"Solid Gospel truth! *Stand Firm With God's Power in Business* provides a clear and concise roadmap for experiencing peace with God and victory as business-based warriors for Christ!"

—*Dr. Charles Fay, President, The Love and Logic Institute, Inc.*

"*Stand Firm With God's Power In Business* is a practical guide to unleash the supernatural power of God in your business and your life! I highly recommend it."

—*Steve Fedyski, President/CEO, Pinnacle Forum*

"Bob Benson's book, *Stand Firm with God's Power in Business*, is an important and enlightening contribution to the literature on leadership. The book presents a compelling case for the importance of integrating our Christian faith into our business practices. The principles in this book provide a powerful framework for orienting all of our work and actions toward Christ. When we view our work through this lens, we begin to see the powerful transformation possible in our organizations and the customers we all strive to serve. Benson provides useful tools, thought-provoking insights, and guided questions designed to assist any organization in repositioning themselves to see their work as Christ's work in our world. I am truly appreciative of the wisdom in this book."

—Amy C. Novak, President, Dakota Wesleyan University

"This book addresses two areas in business that are often overlooked, your work as a mission and our enemy Satan actively seeking to destroy it. Reading *Stand Firm With God's Power in Business* will change the outcome of both."

—Mac Perry, President, Perry & Young, Inc.

"I have seen firsthand what God's power can accomplish in business. *Stand Firm with God's Power in Business* is a primer for focusing that power for long term success."

—Richard K. Reinicke, Vice President, Automotive Warranty Network, Inc.

"Your book really surprised me! It stands out in my mind as possibly one of the top 20 books I've ever read (I've read over 1,000). I'm a constant and continual reader, always looking for relevant and practical information to pass onto others and ways to grow in maturity in my Christian walk and business practice. I look for practical, simple and relevant. The style with which you wrote, the format of the book (which is very simple and easy to follow and digest) was extremely helpful to the eye and the mind to digest and find meaningful content. There was, in my opinion, little or no fluff. For the business person and owner, a lot of practical advice and help. *Stand Firm with God's Power in Business* is not just a book; it is a reference and resource guide that belongs on the desks of all

Christian business owners and on the board room tables when board meetings are held, to be continually consulted for help and advice. We truly don't war against flesh and blood; we war against powers and principalities in the spirit world. We all need the kind of insight you offer/serve up in your book."

—Larry Tyler, CEO, Up Your Business, LLC, Author, ROMANCING the LOAN

"Bob Benson has given us a wonderful addition to the growing teachings that break down the barriers that have existed in the lives of too many Christian business people who have settled for living a dichotomy between their 'faith life' on the weekends, and their 'business life' during the week. As a result, many Christian business people unwittingly place themselves at the mercy of rules of the secular world and the spiritual power behind it – instead of walking in the overcoming victory of the Kingdom of God and the real Spiritual Power behind it. As a former business executive, international missions leader, and Pastor – I highly recommend this powerful and practical 'How To Guide' for Christian business people."

—Pastor Joe Warring, Creekside Bible Church, Aurora, Colorado.

STAND FIRM WITH GOD'S POWER IN BUSINESS

STAND FIRM
WITH GOD'S POWER
IN BUSINESS

HOLD TO HIS TEACHING
WALK IN HIS PROTECTION
LIVE IN HIS BLESSINGS

BOB BENSON

STAND FIRM WITH GOD'S POWER IN BUSINESS

▪ Third Edition ▪

by Bob Benson

Cover and interior design by Lions Roar Studios

All Scriptures in this book are from the New International Version (NIV) of the Bible unless otherwise noted. Other versions used include New Living Translation (NLT), Good New Translation (GNT), Revised Standard Version (RSV) and New King James Version (NKJV).

All bolded quotes of the Bible are for added emphasis only and are not included in the original Scriptures quoted.

DEDICATION

To Ree Ann
my faithful wife, friend,
partner, and helpmate for 52 years;
You are the love of my life.

To my sons, their wives and my grandchildren;
so you might understand
and, as my father taught me,
keep your eyes on Jesus
no matter what struggles or disappointments
you face in this life.

To my brothers and sisters in Christ
working in the business world;
so you might recognize the enemy's schemes
to keep you from holding to God's teaching,
walking in His protection
and living in His blessings.

ACKNOWLEDGMENTS

Everything I know is a summary of God's gifts and what I have learned from Him and the people in my life during the journey that led to writing Stand Firm With God's Power in Business. I have made many mistakes and therefore ask forgiveness from those I may have hurt along the way. We are impacted by many people in our lives and so there are too many for me to recognize individually. You know who you are.

I'm deeply grateful to my wife, Ree Ann. We have been friends or marriage partners since my seventh grade. Thank you for believing in me and supporting me in all my scary entrepreneur ventures. Thank you for teaching me what a real family is. And thank you for loving me and sticking with me through the ups and downs of our marriage. You are special.

My father was a responsible man of few words. I'm eternally grateful he gave his family the awesome heritage of belonging to God's family. And I thank him for teaching me the simple powerful principle of "keep my eyes on Jesus" during life's ups and downs.

I thank all my outstanding pastors and teachers of the Bible for their faithfulness, excellence and sound teaching of God's Word.

Many family members, friends, clients, business partners, business acquaintances, teachers and others have influenced me and the writing of this book in meaningful ways. I am grateful for their encouragement in my life, their belief in me and for all I have learned from them.

I would like to acknowledge Paul Cuny, Steve Fedyski and Joe Warring for their encouragement to write this book and support in writing it, as well as Jeff and Dawn Clark at Stromata Enterprises for assistance in editing it.

And a special thank you to my Father in Heaven for His love, mercy and grace, the Lord Jesus Christ for His leadership and power and the Holy Spirit for His counsel and insights.

CONTENTS

FORWARD

Bob Benson's book, *Stand Firm with God's Power in Business*, is a treasure waiting for you to unearth. This book addresses a common misconception globally among Christians in the business world today. Most people working in business I have met around the world believe that only pastors, missionaries and people in vocational ministry are experiencing the opposition of Satan - the enemy of our souls. This is one of the unintended consequences of the sacred/secular mindset and it has produced a generation of Christians who are ill-equipped to operate in the full rights of citizenship of the Kingdom.

God is raising up many men and women in our day with a depth of understanding of the Scriptures, combined with a breath of practical experience, who are destroying this myth. Bob Benson is one of those men. Bob explains that the enemy will always oppose building of churches or sending missionaries, but he doesn't stop there. Satan opposes everything God endorses – a business dedicated to functioning on Kingdom principles, a church in Africa or person sharing the Gospel with a co-worker. He opposes a missionary to Central America, but he also will vigorously oppose a Kingdom minded business leader in Brazil who employs 200 families.

Stand Firm with God's Power in Business will equip you with one of the missing ingredients, a solid, balanced understanding of one of the keys for success of any business venture – knowledge of the schemes of the enemy of our soul. I have read many books on spiritual warfare, but this is the first one I have seen that is written for people in the business world by a business leader. *Stand Firm with God's Power in Business* is written by a man who has spent his life helping hundreds of business owners/leaders understand the culture that produces the blessings of God on the business they are caretakers over. Bob is not giving us theory, but Biblically based, practical solutions that have been developed from over 40 years of observing himself and other business owners/leaders make the same mistakes, ignore the same principles, and overlook the same critical success factors of the Kingdom economy. Finally, Bob decided to write this book to share these God breathed insights with a larger audience.

The insights in *Stand Firm with God's Power in Business* will change your life. Bob reveals these God given insights in a methodical manner that is consistent with a teacher's anointing and the desire to see men and women live in victory and freedom. This is a very well written book that is filled with practical life examples that will move your life and business career from the mundane to the extraordinary, from defeat to victory.

Stand Firm with God's Power in Business will produce in you a desire for a single minded pursuit of God and His presence. You can find through the pages of this book, a deeper intimacy with God than you have ever known. This book will help you discover that you serve a 7 day a week God, who cares about every detail of your life Monday through Saturday, as well as Sunday! I pray you will begin a complete understanding through *Stand Firm with God's Power in Business,* that you are fully equipped as a citizen of the Kingdom of God to live the life of an overcomer. Bob Benson is going to take you on a life changing journey through the pages of this book.

Paul L. Cuny, President,

MarketPlace Leadership International

Author, *Secrets of the Kingdom Economy*

INTRODUCTION

The LORD **was with** *Joseph, so he succeeded in everything he did as he served in the home of his Egyptian master.*
Genesis 39:2 NLT

How would you like to have God "with you" as you work in the business world? The Bible says when you choose to live life God's way by following His commands and teachings, His power is with you. If you obey God, it says He will bless the work of your hands (your career). *The Lord will send a blessing on your barns and on everything you put your hand to* (Deuteronomy 28:8a).

God walked with Joseph and many others in Scripture who obeyed Him, including Moses, David, Enoch, Noah, Abraham, Hannah, Jacob, Joshua, Deborah, Elijah, Elisha, Jeremiah, John, Mary, Paul, Lydia, Apollos, Peter and so on. God gives us their stories in the Bible as object lessons concerning how to walk with Him at all times. He was with them, and gave them favor because they followed His ways. All of these individuals are just normal people, like you and me. Most of the Apostles of Christ came from the business domain of their day. As a matter of fact, Jesus' father and His family were in business as carpenters.

Under the New Covenant, the Lord Jesus Christ also says the Father will be with those who obey Him and He will walk with them providing supernatural protection and blessings in their lives.

> *I am the vine; you are the branches. If you remain in Me and I in you, you will bear much fruit; apart from Me you can do nothing. If you do not remain in Me, you are like a branch that is thrown away and withers; such branches are picked up, thrown into the fire and burned. If you remain in Me and My words remain in you, ask whatever you wish, and it will be done for you. This is to My Father's glory, that you bear much fruit, showing yourselves to be My disciples.*
>
> *As the Father has loved Me, so have I loved you. Now remain in My love. If you keep My commands, you will remain in My love, just as I have kept My Father's commands and remain in His love (John 15:5-10).*

Do you want God with you during your entire career so you can continuously walk in His protection and live in His blessings? Then the Scripture says to hold to His teaching with the confidence that He will be with you. *Have I not commanded you? Be strong and courageous. Do not be afraid; do not be discouraged, for the Lord your God will be with you wherever you go (Joshua 1:9).*

What seems to have been nearly forgotten in Christianity is that the Bible also says we have an enemy who has schemes to tempt and manipulate Christians from following God's commands and teaching. If successful, this disobedience damages our relationship with God and His <u>full</u> blessing and protection are no longer on our lives.

> *Then war broke out in heaven. Michael and his angels fought*

against the dragon, and the dragon and his angels fought back. But he was not strong enough, and they lost their place in heaven. The great dragon was hurled down—that ancient serpent called the devil, or Satan, who leads the whole world astray. He was hurled to the earth, and his angels with him. Then the dragon was enraged at the woman and went off to wage war against the rest of her offspring—those who keep God's commands and hold fast their testimony about Jesus (Revelation 12:7-9, 17).

One morning, as I was shaving, a thought came to my mind, "God doesn't care about your business." Already struggling with some discouragement, the thought that God didn't care about my business' success or failure nearly overwhelmed me. As I contemplated this thought, some depression began to set in. The more I gave ground to this thought, the more I began to believe it.

I had been studying the idea of Satan communicating with us in our minds for months. Suddenly the light came on for me as I realized what was going on. In that instant, I knew exactly how to respond. "That's not true Satan!" I replied. "The Bible says *'I know the plans I have for you,' declares the Lord, 'plans to prosper you and not to harm you, plans to give you a hope and a future.'* So go away, Satan!" I declared in the name of Jesus. Instantly, my mind became completely peaceful. The agitation was gone, the depression was gone...all of it. I was at peace in my heart. But Satan would return to try again!

Few Christians can dispute the fact that we face daily battles similar to the one I just described to you. There is no question in the Bible as to who is waging this battle against us: Satan, the fallen angel - the enemy of God and His creation.

One of Satan's primary strategic targets is the marketplace

– **the business domain!** Why? Because those who work in the marketplace and own businesses have significant influence over most of the population. The marketplace is where they spend the majority of their time, so that is where the enemy intensifies his attacks. Of additional concern to the enemy is that business people are also most likely to have the resources to promote and advance the Kingdom of God on earth. Unfortunately, most Christians working in the marketplace are easy prey for Satan because they are unaware of his schemes and the subtlety of his participation in their lives and minds (John 10:3-5).

In her devotional *Jesus Calling*, Sarah Young reminds us that, "There is a MIGHTY BATTLE going on for control of your mind. Heaven and earth intersect in your mind; the tugs of both spheres influence your thinking."

Most people who work in business do not see their work as a holy calling. And the enemy likes it that way. The renowned philosophy professor, speaker and author, Dallas Willard, said, "It is as great and as difficult a spiritual calling to run the factories and the mines, the banks and the department stores, the schools and government agencies for the Kingdom of God as it is to pastor a church or serve as an evangelist."

Michael Baer, a businessman and former pastor, in his book *Business as Mission*, says that, "In much of the world there is a fundamental conviction among sincere Christians that there is something intrinsically wrong with business and no serious follower of Christ would go into business, much less consider it a calling." Nothing could be further from the truth! Baer goes on to say, "Business is a good thing from God…a high calling from God." You may sense such a calling on your life and already view your job or business as a ministry. More likely, you may be wondering if you can really be "doing something for God" while working in a business.

Baer points out that God "is a God of purpose and plans, that He has an end in mind for the things He does and creates." The Bible teaches us that we each have a purpose: *In Him we were also chosen, having been predestined according to the plan of Him who works out everything in conformity with the purpose of His will* (Ephesians 1:11). *For we are God's handiwork, created in Christ Jesus to do good works, which God prepared in advance for us to do* (Ephesians 2:10).

In the middle of fulfilling God's purpose for your life, you are in the middle of this cosmic war! A real-life melodrama! The cast of characters are: God and His forces of good; Satan (also known as the devil) and his forces of darkness; and mankind. Sound weird? I used to think so, too.

Proof of this spiritual battle is well documented by facts. Professor Bradley Wright, a sociologist at the University of Connecticut, explains that from his analysis of people who identify themselves as Christians but rarely attend church, 60% of them have been divorced. Of those who attend church regularly, 38% have been divorced [1]. Further, 51% of pastors say cyber-pornography is a possible temptation, 37% say it is a current struggle [2].

Approximately 47% of Christians state that pornography is a major problem in their home [3]. And, while polling data on pornography use among adults remains unclear and varying, a ChristiaNet poll finds that as many as 50% of Christian men and

---

1 Bradley R.E. Wright, "Christians Are Hate-Filled Hypocrites ...and Other Lies You've Been Told," (Minneapolis, MN: Bethany House, 2010), p. 133

2 Christianity Today, Leadership Survey, 12/200

3 Pornography Statistics, Family Safe Media (2007)

20% of Christian women could be addicted to pornography [4].

Satan knows that each one of us has been knit together in our mother's womb (Psalm 139:13) and that God has called each of us to such a time as this (Esther 4:14). In other words, God has created each of us for a specific purpose at a specific time. Satan will do whatever he can to stop God's purposes!

"Do you want to accept a challenge that will be the integrating dynamic of your whole life? One that will engage your loftiest thoughts, your most dedicated exertions, your deepest emotions, all your abilities and resources, to the last step you take and the last breath you breathe? Listen to Jesus of Nazareth; ANSWER HIS CALL." - Os Guinness, *The Call*

Every calling, whether pastor or plumber, is a high calling from God and the Spirit of Truth lives in each believer in Christ!

While I have taken no seminary courses nor hold a theological degree, I do have an advanced degree from the school of hard knocks and the spiritual war in business. We have observed with amazement as the Lord has watched over and blessed Ree Ann and me for 52 years since our marriage in high school. In spite of me, the Holy Spirit has carefully and purposefully guided us through this journey during our lives. And for a long time I wondered in puzzlement how an average kid from a small town in Nebraska could successfully build businesses. I would like to share with you some very powerful insights He has taught me in this journey.

By the way, there is nothing special about me or my ability

4 ChristianNet Poll Finds That Evangelicals Are Addicted to Porn Market Wire, 7 August 2006

to learn these things. The Bible says that the Holy Spirit (the Counselor) will "lead you to all truth" if you follow Christ and hold to His teaching. If I can do it, anyone can!

According to the Bible, God loves us and wants us to live life to the fullest. *"I know the plans I have for you," declares the Lord. "plans to prosper you and not to harm you, plans to give you hope and a future"* (Jeremiah 29:11). About now many of you may be thinking, "Really? God has such a plan for MY life?" Absolutely, He does!

Prior to this journey, I was pretty sheltered and naive. Little did I know that this spiritual war can impact a person's beliefs, decisions, morals and their consequences! Little did I know it can impact a person physically, emotionally and spiritually! Little did I know it can impact a person's family and relationships! Little did I know it could impact a person's success in school, at work or in any domain of life! Little did I know, that as a business man, it could impact my job or my business! Little did I know it could impact my protection and blessings from God! LITTLE did I know!

To overcome Satan's schemes, the Apostle Paul instructs Christians to, *Put on the full armor of God so that you can take your stand against the devil's schemes. For our struggle is not against flesh and blood* (people - including yourself), *but against the rulers, against the authorities, against the powers of this dark world and against the spiritual forces of evil in the heavenly realms. Therefore put on the full armor of God, so that when the day of evil comes, you may be able to stand your ground, and after you have done everything, to stand* (Ephesians 6:10-13).

Note that he doesn't say "if" the day of evil comes, he says "when." I will explain in this book how to recognize the devil's schemes and defeat him and his forces of darkness by putting on the

full armor of God in the marketplace so you **stand firm** with God's Power.

As you read my book and apply what you learn, you will discover practical ways to use the Armor daily. And if you persevere, you will overcome Satan and his forces of darkness. How am I so sure of this? It is the Word of God!

It doesn't matter what religion you believe in or whether you believe in God, or Satan, at all. It doesn't matter what nationality you are. It doesn't matter what color your skin is or what sex you are. If you're a human being, Satan has already impacted every aspect of your life, and will continue to attempt to do so. To overcome him, you must learn to recognize this reality and be positioned, equipped and empowered to stand against him.

You may think this war with Satan and his forces of darkness doesn't apply to you. Everything is running smoothly in your life. You're not a bad person. You are moral and honest. You haven't killed anyone. You don't steal from people. Well, the "day of evil" Paul talks about doesn't need to be some horrible action, event or crisis in your life. It can be as simple as Satan influencing you to be self-focused, resulting in frequent frustration or anger with people. It could be disobeying the Lord's commandment to "make disciples" and/or love one another - especially with those who irritate you or have done you wrong.

If you believe you have no need to be educated in this spiritual war, then Satan has already won the battle with you. In fact, he has already deceived much of the Church into complacency. According to a recent study by Lifeway Research, 61% of American Protestant church attendees have never shared how to become a Christian with anyone. Yet 75% say they feel comfortable sharing their Christian beliefs and a full 80% believe they have a personal responsibility to share the gospel with non-Christians! Some argue that "Thou shalt witness to thy neighbor" cannot be found in the Ten Commandments, so we don't need to do it. Nonetheless, the Bible gives all Christians a clear mandate to make disciples and it is obvious that Satan has had a great measure of success in suppressing the spreading of the gospel and making of disciples by the Church. In so doing, he has succeeded in making the Body of Christ dysfunctional.

I pray this book will bless you and yours!

**"THE THIEF COMES ONLY TO STEAL,
AND KILL, AND DESTROY;
I CAME THAT THEY MAY HAVE LIFE,
AND HAVE IT ABUNDANTLY."**

The Lord Jesus Christ

Jesus replied,
"Very truly I tell you,
no one can see
the Kingdom of God
unless they are
born again."

John 3:3

CHAPTER 1

REAL CHRISTIANITY –
ITS IMPORTANCE IN KEEPING GOD WITH YOU

Understanding the spiritual war with the forces of darkness begins with an understanding of Real Christianity. Real Christianity is about establishing a relationship with God as His child, not joining a religion. Regardless of what church, denomination or religion you do or do not belong to, what sex you are or what race you are, if you are interested in growing spiritually, experiencing life abundantly on earth (as declared by Jesus Christ), receiving eternal life as a gift from God and successfully defeating Satan's schemes, then understanding Real Christianity is imperative to your success!

Many "intellectuals" in educational institutions and others across the world today would have you believe there is no God or that He is not personal and involved in your daily life. However, one of the most brilliant intellectuals of all time, Albert Einstein, clearly believed in God. Any intellectually honest person who examines the facts surrounding the function of the universe has to come to "a rapturous amazement at the harmony of natural law" (to quote

Einstein) and must conclude that God exists. Anyone who does not, according to Scripture, is a fool (Psalms 14:1). Therefore, let us examine together the truth about God, man's dilemma, why God's solution to man's dilemma is designed the way it is, and how to spend eternity with Him in His Kingdom.

The Bible says that life on this earth is short. *All people are like grass and all their faithfulness is like the flowers of the field; the grass withers and the flowers fall, but the word of our God endures forever* (Isaiah 40:6&8).

Scripture also says that seeking God His way results in a person receiving a new indestructible body in the next life that is "raised in strength": *Our bodies are buried in brokenness, but they will be raised in glory. They are buried in weakness, but they will be raised in strength* (1 Corinthians 15:43 NLT).

As you can see, the most important question in your short lifetime on this earth is: What are you going to believe about God, Jesus Christ, eternal life and life here on earth? The Bible says receiving eternal life from God grants you the rights of being a member of His family, an imperishable spiritual body in the next life, and, starting here on earth, the benefits of being a citizen of His Kingdom. Real Christianity offers you the free gift of eternal life through an act of God's grace and freedom from the tyranny of your sinful nature while living on earth. In all other religions, you must earn and work your way to Heaven - a mission impossible! For those who want to be a real Christian, though, the Bible says *The work of God is this: to believe in the One He has sent* (John 6:29).

The Apostle Peter sums up the process of spiritual growth after you believe in Jesus Christ this way: *In view of all this, make every effort to respond to God's promises. Supplement your faith with a generous provision of moral excellence, and moral excellence with knowledge, and knowledge with self-control, and self-control with patient endurance, and patient endurance with godliness, and godliness with brotherly affection, and brotherly affection with love for everyone. The more you grow like this, the more productive and useful you will be in your knowledge of our Lord Jesus Christ* (2 Peter 1:5-8 NLT). Rather than working and earning our way to Heaven, Peter tells us to apply the promises and let God grow us into spiritual maturity. For the Apostle Paul tells us in his writings that only God creates this spiritual growth in you, so that you are dependent on daily faith in Jesus Christ to complete the spiritual growth process referred to in Christianity as sanctification.

THE CONDITION WITH OUR HUMAN BODIES

Humans, all humans, have a fatal condition. This condition is called "sin." You may think sin is only a verb, something a person does. The word is often used that way, but in the Bible, the Apostle Paul frequently uses the word sin as a noun – something *living in* him. As it is, this sin living in you is passed from generation to generation, all the way from Generation One - Adam and Eve! And, it creates weaknesses in every person's human nature - referred to by Paul as the sinful nature (meaning a nature that can't help sinning).

The Greek philosopher, Plato, said, "If you would converse with me, please, first, define your terms." So first, let's define the verb sin. Dummies.com defines it thusly: "Sin is any deliberate action, attitude, or thought that goes against God and His commands. You may think of sin as an obvious act, such as murder, marital unfaithfulness or theft. Although that's true, sin is also wrongdoing that's far subtler and even unnoticeable at times, such as pride, envy or even worry. Sin includes not only things you shouldn't have done, but did (sins of commission), it also includes things you should've done, but didn't (sins of omission)." The Online Dictionary defines sin as: "A transgression of a religious or moral law, especially when deliberate...Deliberate disobedience to the known will of God...A condition of estrangement from God resulting from such disobedience." Furthermore, the Bible says that disobeying God is sin regardless of whether you know it is sin or not (Leviticus 4). Like breaking laws established by earthly authorities, ignorance of the law is not a defense against breaking a law. For example, officers and directors of a corporation may not know they can be held personally liable (both civilly and criminally) for failing to properly withhold and remit payroll taxes to the IRS. This fact is irrelevant, however, if the IRS decides to pursue those remedies in a court of law.

And who among mankind can claim they have never broken one of God's laws – the Ten Commandments? *For all have sinned and fall short of the glory of God* (Romans 3:23). Obviously no-one!

These definitions are traditional and represent how most people think about sin – as something that we do or don't do. But there is something more important to understand about the word sin! As we just discussed, the Bible also uses the word *sin* as a noun, to describe a thing, living in you, resulting in a condition called a "sinful nature," sin living in your human nature which you can't control!

This simple but profound insight about the word "sin" (which I learned after being a Christian for over 20 years) transformed my understanding of the Bible, clarified better what Jesus Christ did at the cross, and helped set me free. The Apostle Paul confirms the truth of this condition in Romans 7:20, *Now if I do what I do not want to do, it is no longer I who do it, but it is sin living in me that does it.*

So the next time you say to yourself or others, "I don't understand why (fill in the name) does those things," now you know why!

How did humans get into this dilemma? Let's look at a summary of events from the Bible:

» **First, God created humans without any flaws.** God created mankind in His own image, in the image of God He created them; male and female He created them... God saw all that He had made, and it was very good (Genesis 1:27&31).

» **Second, God gave Adam and Eve a command to protect their life and preserve their perfect nature.** The LORD God took the man and put him in the Garden of Eden to work it and take care of it. *And the LORD God commanded the man, 'You are free to eat from any tree in the garden; but you must not eat from the tree of the* ***knowledge of good and evil*** *for when you eat from it you will certainly die (physically and spiritually)'* (Genesis 2:15-17).

» **Third, the devil, God's enemy, tempted man to disobey God.** *He said to the woman, 'Did God really say, 'You must not eat from any tree in the garden?' The woman said to the serpent, 'We may eat fruit from the trees in the garden, but God did say, 'You must not eat fruit from the tree that is in the middle of the garden, and you must not touch it, or you will die.' 'You will not certainly die,' the serpent said to the woman. 'For God knows that when you eat from it your eyes will be opened, and you will be like God, knowing good and evil'* (Genesis 3:1-5).

» **Fourth, man disobeyed God.** *When the woman saw that the fruit of the tree was good for food and pleasing to the eye, and also desirable for gaining wisdom, she took some and ate it. She also gave some to her husband, who was with her, and he ate it* (Genesis 3:6).

» **Fifth, because of their disobedience, sin (the noun) entered man.** *Then the eyes of both of them were opened, and they realized they were naked; so they sewed fig leaves* *together and made coverings for themselves* (Genesis 3:7).

- **Sixth, because sin (the noun) was now living in man, they were no longer allowed to live in God's Kingdom,** *so they were banished from it: And the LORD God said, 'The man has now become like one of Us, knowing good and evil. He must not be allowed to reach out his hand and take also from the tree of life and eat, and live forever.' So the LORD God banished him from the Garden of Eden to work the ground from which he had been taken. After He drove the man out, He placed on the east side of the Garden of Eden cherubim and a flaming sword flashing back and forth to guard the way to the tree of life* (Genesis 3:22-24).
- **Seventh, sin (the noun) was passed from generation to generation in all humans.** *Sin entered the world through one man, and death through sin, and in this way death came to all people* (Romans 5:12).

There is only one solution for this sin condition in our human nature. The Bible says that, *all have sinned and fall short of the glory of God* (Romans 3:23) and that *the wages of sin is death, but the gift of God is eternal life in Christ Jesus our Lord* (Romans 6:23). As most estate planners point out, the mortality rate in this life is 100%. So which death and life is the Apostle Paul, author of Romans, talking about? He is talking of spiritual death (separation from God and His life-giving power for eternity) and spiritual life (unity and fellowship with God and connectedness to His life-giving power for eternity). Connection to God is what gives a person the feeling of life: love, joy, peace, goodness, etc. – a feeling of well-being and safety, including the absence of fear, violence and hatred. Disconnection from God produces an environment of the opposite characteristics, because all love and goodness flows only from God. There is no other source to obtain them!

GOD'S SOLUTION FOR OUR CONDITION

No one escapes the reality of physical death on this earth. Remember the 100% mortality rate? However, the Bible does say a person can escape spiritual death and regain life everlasting! The critical question is "how?"

As we saw in Romans 7:17&20, sin is a noun - something that is living in us. So, was Paul trying to avoid responsibility by saying we are all possessed by some sin-committing alien? No! Put in context, he is using his own experience to define reality for us and help each person understand the helplessness of their condition apart from accepting Christ's death at the Cross as payment for his or her sins.

As you study the book of Romans, you see that Paul is also teaching us that through daily faith in Jesus Christ, the sin living in us is rendered powerless through daily faith in Christ. *Who will rescue me from this body that is subject to death? Thanks be to God – through Jesus Christ our Lord!* (Romans 7:24-25) The sin living in you creates what the Bible calls a sinful nature and that is why it says that all have sinned. With sin-living in you, it is impossible for you not to sin. However, God is a God of justice, mercy and grace. He has always had a plan in place for humans to be set free from their sinful nature. God gave His Son Jesus Christ, King of His Kingdom, to come to earth and to die in your place to pay the penalty of death for your sins and to provide a solution for rendering your sinful nature powerless through daily faith in Christ!

You may be thinking this all sounds very strange and wonder, as many have over the centuries, "Why did Christ have to come to earth and die?" As our Creator, couldn't God "just fix it"? Or why couldn't Jesus just come to earth and 'Wow' us into believing in Him? To answer this, let's first examine what's different about Christianity from other religions.

Of the world's adult population, 33% list Christianity as their religion. In the U.S., it's 76%. Why is Christianity so prevalent? Because Christianity is the only religion that promises to set you free from your sinful nature and give you eternal life in Heaven through an act of God's grace by believing in His Son Jesus Christ. Remember, in all other religions, YOU must control your behavior and work your way to Heaven!

It also does not matter if you were raised in a Christian home or attend a Christian church. Those are good things, but they do not make you a Christian. Going to church without God living in you is just being religious. God, through His Spirit, comes to live in you when you become a child of God.

Real Christianity as explained in the Bible is not a religion; it is a personal relationship with God by becoming His child. God is a personal being and wants to be personally involved in your life. Jesus replied, *"Anyone who loves Me will obey My teaching. My Father will love them, and We will come to them and make Our home with them."* (John 14:23). Christ taught us in John, chapter 3, how to start this relationship. In reply, Jesus declared, *'I tell you the truth, no one can see the Kingdom of God unless they are born again.' That is, born of... the Spirit (of God). Flesh gives birth to flesh, but the Spirit gives birth to spirit (your spirit). For God so loved the world that He gave His one and only Son, that whoever believes in Him shall not perish but have eternal life* (John 3:3,5,6,16).

You become a child of God when you invite His Son Jesus Christ into your life as Savior and Lord. Then, as you begin to spend time with Him, He becomes more real and personal with you on a daily basis.

The Bible has much to say about how to establish and maintain such a relationship with God, including the benefits of the relationship. When a person puts their belief in Jesus Christ, that person is born into God's family. It is at that time your relationship with God's family begins: *Yet to all who did receive Him* (Christ), *to those who believed in His name, He gave the right to become children of God - children born not of natural descent, nor of human decision or a husband's will, but born of God* (John 1:12-13). That is, your spirit is given life as was intended from the beginning of creation and God lives in you (your spirit) for eternity, regardless of what kind of physical body (flesh or imperishable) your spirit lives in!

Real Christianity is all founded on being born again, that is, being born into God's family. Consider the following dialogue of this subject by the Son of God:

Jesus answered, 'I am telling you the truth: no one can see the Kingdom of God without being born again. 'How can a grown man be born again?' Nicodemus asked. 'He certainly cannot enter his mother's womb and be born a second time!' 'I am telling you the truth,' replied Jesus, 'that no one can enter the Kingdom of God without being born of water and the Spirit. A person is born physically of human parents, but is born spiritually of the Spirit (John 3:3-6 GNT).

For God so loved the world that He gave His one and only Son, that whoever believes in Him shall not perish but have eternal life. For God did not send His Son into the world to condemn the world, but to save the world through Him (John 3:16-17).

What the Son of God is explaining here is that the only way to Heaven is to be born into God's family. Then and only then, can a person understand that he or she has received eternal life through a work of God's grace, by belief in Jesus Christ. The only way to receive this gift is by believing in and trusting Jesus Christ! Rejection of God's gift will result in separation from God's life-giving power for eternity. And until you accept God's gift by faith, you can neither receive it nor even understand it!

When you accept this free gift from God, Christ will set you free from the sin living in you, *Therefore, there is now no condemnation for those who are in Christ Jesus, because through Christ Jesus the law of the Spirit Who gives life has set you free from the law of sin and death* (Romans 8:1-2).

Then, through **daily** faith in Christ, He continues to render the sin nature powerless. *I have been crucified with Christ* (when He died for my sins at the cross) *and I no longer live, but Christ lives in me. The life I now live in the body* (my physical body with a sinful nature), *I live by faith in the Son of God, who loved me and gave Himself for me. I do not set aside the grace of God, for if righteousness could be gained through the law, Christ died for nothing* (Galatians 2:20-21)!

ANOTHER KEY BENEFIT OF REAL CHRISTIANITY

The Apostle Paul explains to believers in Christ that as Adam brought death into the world by sinning, Jesus brings resurrection from the dead by defeating sin. We all die because of our relationship to Adam. Likewise, we all receive new eternal life and a new heavenly body suitable for the Kingdom because of our relationship with Christ.

But someone will ask, 'How are the dead raised? With what kind of body will they come?'" How foolish! There are also heavenly bodies, and there are earthly bodies; but the splendor of the heavenly bodies is one kind, and the splendor of the earthly bodies is another. So will it be with the resurrection of the dead. The body that is sown is perishable, it is raised imperishable (1 Corinthians 15:35, 40, 42).

So indeed, we will have a body in the next life, but it will be of a different nature - or "glory" - and will never die! Paul goes on: *it is sown in dishonor, it is raised in glory; it is sown in weakness, it is raised in power; it is sown a natural body, it is raised a spiritual body. If there is a natural body, there is also a spiritual body* (1 Corinthians 15:43-44).

Paul continues to clarify: *I declare to you, brothers and sisters, that flesh and blood cannot inherit the kingdom of God, nor does the perishable inherit the imperishable. For the perishable must clothe itself with the imperishable, and the mortal with immortality* (1 Corinthians 15:50, 53). The significance, Paul points out to us, is that Adam's body was created from the dust of the earth, for life on earth, and so must return to the earth. But for the believers in Christ, those earthly bodies are raised to become imperishable, incorruptible bodies which are suitable for life in God's Kingdom, because they came from Heaven.

Let me explain using an example from the business world. Let's assume you purchase a new, state of the art, highly advanced computer equipment system with a very powerful and extremely superior operating and network system. All its hardware, software and systems operate perfectly and have been proven flawless in their internal environment and functions. There is only one condition to sustaining its exceptional perfection. Only equipment and software made and approved by its manufacturer can be connected to and allowed to enter into its highly advanced network. No exceptions!

Yes, our earthly bodies do disappoint us. They are weak, sickly, and dysfunctional. And they get weaker, sicker and more dysfunctional as they age. Eventually they die. So who does the Bible say can be set free from their body of sin here on earth, receive eternal life and have new heavenly bodies - bodies that are imperishable, never get sick and never die? The Bible says it is those who have faith in God by believing in and putting their trust in His Son Jesus Christ, the *only begotten Son of God (the radiance of God's glory and the exact representation of His being* - Hebrews 1:3) .

If you have not already done so, you can become a child of God right now by receiving Him into your life.

CHOOSE LIFE

Hopefully I have given you a clearer and more practical understanding of Christianity – Real Christianity. We all know that some decisions in life are significantly more important than others. So ask yourself these questions: Can I honestly stand before God someday and claim I have never broken His law, The Ten Commandments? How do I know I will go to Heaven and get an imperishable body after I die? On what basis do I know for sure? If your answers are not consistent with the path to eternal life the Son of God has outlined above, you have three choices:

- » Begin a personal relationship with God by becoming His child by faith - admitting to Jesus Christ that you have sinned against God, thanking Jesus for dying on the cross as payment for your sins, inviting Him into your life as your Savior and Lord and following His teachings.
- » Choose not to believe what you learned in this chapter.
- » Check out Real Christianity further. In this case, I recommend you start attending a church that teaches and preaches from the Bible on a weekly basis.

The Bible says once you become a "born again" Christian, you become a member of God's royal family. Therefore, you inherit a birthright which I explain in Chapter 2 and you are assured of (cannot lose) your eternal life with God in His Kingdom:

- *And this is the testimony: God has given us eternal life, and this life is in His Son. Whoever has the Son has life; whoever does not have the Son of God does not have life* (1 John 5:11-12).
- *Now it is God who makes both us and you stand firm in Christ. He anointed us, set His seal of ownership on us, and put His Spirit in our hearts as a deposit, guaranteeing what is to come* (2 Corinthians 1:21-22).

NOW CHOOSE LIFE, SO THAT YOU...

MAY LIVE AND THAT YOU MAY LOVE THE LORD YOUR GOD,

LISTEN TO HIS VOICE, AND HOLD FAST TO HIM.

FOR THE LORD IS YOUR LIFE.

Moses

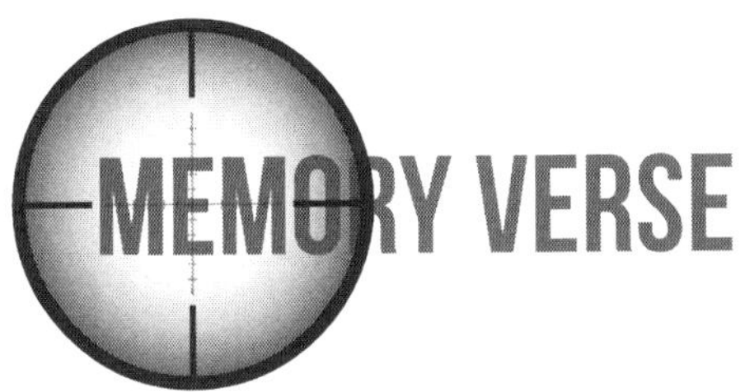

Yet to all who did receive Him, to those who believed in His name, He gave the right to become children of God— children born not of natural descent, nor of human decision or a husband's will, but born of God.

John 1:12-13

QUESTIONS FOR CONSIDERATION:

- What is the "condition" living in every person?
- What is God's solution for this condition?
- What is Real Christianity?
- How does one become a real Christian? How does one know he/she is a real Christian?
- What decision have you made about being born again and becoming a child of God, the Father?
- What are the benefits of being born again? How will they impact your career and/or business?

But you are a chosen people, a royal priesthood, a holy nation, God's special possession, that you may declare the praises of Him who called you out of darkness into His wonderful light. Once you were not a people, but now you are the people of God...

1 Peter 2:9-10

CHAPTER 2

YOUR IDENTITY IN CHRIST AND THE BUSINESS CONNECTION

When you think about yourself, how do you define your identity? Do you define yourself as "My name is…, I am male/female, my nationality is…, my father and mother are …, I am a citizen of…, I grew up in…, I do… for a living, I am the spouse of…, I am a father/mother of…children, my brothers and sisters are…, I am attractive/not so attractive, etc." Or, is it "I am a child of God - the Father Almighty in Heaven. Christ is my brother, all of God's children are my brothers and sisters. I am a citizen of the Kingdom of God – a holy nation, I am a joint heir with Christ, and Jesus Christ is my King"? As a born again Christian, the latter is how God sees you. He sees the reality of who you are. You are His child!

Your true identity and birthright is under attack by Satan and his forces of darkness. As you live life, facing its ups and downs and seeking the desires of your heart, do you really know your true identity? Do you know who you are? A true Christian is reborn supernaturally into the family of God. Accordingly, He is your Father in the spiritual world – the invisible world, of which your spirit (the real you) is a part. And Jesus Christ is not only your Savior, He is King of the government of that world, known as the Kingdom of God. The Bible says that as His child you are a citizen of that Kingdom and therefore, He is your King. You are under His protection and are joint heirs with Him - under God's Covenant Promise - to all the rights, blessings and heritage that come with it. In 1 John 3:1, the Apostle John considers this an awesome reality and is very intentional about proclaiming how special it is to be a child of God: *See what great love the Father has lavished on us, that we should be called children of God! And that is what we are!*

MY PERSONAL JOURNEY

I became a child of God in 1957, at the age of 13, while attending the Billy Sunday Memorial Tabernacle in Sioux City, Iowa. My parents were divorced and dad had remarried a divorced woman with twin daughters. So my sister and I started a new journey with them. Dad and my stepmother had decided there must be more to life than the party style living that led to their divorces. After some searching, they found a church that explained to them what Real Christianity was and they each made the decision to invite Christ into their lives as Savior and Lord. Our new family traveled back and forth every Sunday from a small town in eastern Nebraska where we lived. The pastor was an excellent teacher and I learned some very important truths, but obviously wasn't growing into a very mature Christian, as evidenced by the fact that my wife and I married and had a child in high school.

This event in Ree Ann and my lives was viewed by all as a very bad situation and destined for certain failure, but God used it for good. As I look back over our life together, I am certain that from the very moment Ree Ann (who was born into God's family shortly before we married) and I committed to marry and have the child we created, God was with us! For the next 26 years - except for four years of college and three years after college while I went through a somewhat typical phase of rebellion against Christianity - I lived a traditional life as a committed Christian, going to excellent churches and Sunday schools, reading the Bible and Christian books. During this time I received sound teaching from the Bible by my pastors and others in the Christian religion. But something was missing.

In 1983, I found myself in a puzzling situation. Despite being an elder at one of the ten fastest growing churches in America, Chairman of the Board of a Denver youth ministry, married to a beautiful woman who I loved very much (and still do!) and a co-founder and managing partner of a very successful local CPA firm - I was miserable inside! I wondered why the Lord wouldn't answer my prayers to take away the emotional pain inside of me.

To make life even more puzzling, I observed the lack of agreement in fundamental Christian denominations over what the Bible says is truth. I was shocked by some of the behavior I had experienced and observed in Christianity and the lack of integrity by several Christians in the marketplace, as well as some Christian organizations I was familiar with. I was also amazed at the open tolerance of disobedience to God in Christianity. All of this was troubling to me. But most troubling to me was some of my own behavior.

I cried out to the Lord with questions, "What is going on in Christianity? What is going on inside of me? Why am I in so much emotional pain when everything seems to be going well in my life? Why is there so much 'legalism' and lack of love in the Church and in the new Christian family my father and stepmother have made? Why is there so much confusion in Christianity over what the 'truth' is? After all, the Bible says: *The words of the wise are like goads, their collected sayings like firmly embedded nails* – ***given by One Shepherd*** (Ecclesiastes 12:11). 'One Shepherd,' Lord. That's You! And You teach everyone the same truth! You are the same yesterday, today and tomorrow. So why do I get a lot of double talk when I ask the religious community tough questions? What is going on? What is the problem? What is the truth? What is the solution?"

"Bob," the Lord spoke to me in my mind, "if you want to know the truth, you are not going to find it in any one denomination or church. You need to look for it everywhere. This doesn't mean you should stop going to church. You need to go to church and learn from your pastors and teachers. But your primary teacher must be Me! I will lead you to the truth as they speak, as you read the Bible and as you use other sources. I teach you. But, your primary source for learning the truth is the Bible, so make it your reading priority." In other words, He was telling me to "chew up the meat and spit out the bones" as I trust Him as the source of truth – *given by One Shepherd.*

Then He told me to, "Do a word search in the Bible of the word 'truth.'" There were no easy-to-use computer software or search engines available to me in those days, so I got out a big concordance we had laying around the house. Hours later, I had looked up all the references! Through that process the Lord gave me some powerful insights and I put them together in an unpublished Bible study called, *The Truth Will Set You Free.* I didn't know it at the time, but I was just getting started learning the answers to my questions.

During this search I found Bible verses that changed my life forever – some of them very straightforward, but controversial enough to make many religious leaders squirm and avoid them. Here's an example: *When He, the Spirit of truth, comes, He will guide you into all the truth* (John 16:13). *"All truth,'* that's a mind blowing statement," I thought, and the Lord says it repeatedly in John 14-16. But, the Lord had just answered my prayer and shown me the gateway to truth. So, I decided to believe Scripture and I asked the Holy Spirit to lead me to the truth about what was going on.

The first thing the Holy Spirit did was counsel me that I needed to make some changes in my own life. I agreed and declared that I would change some of my behavior and began shedding beliefs and behavior I picked up in the world. At that very moment it was as if my life was turned upside down and as they say, "all hell broke loose." I found myself in the middle of something I had never experienced – intense spiritual attacks by the forces of darkness! I was under attack, my business was under attack and my family was under attack.

The enemy didn't like my new declaration to be intentional about obeying God and learning the truth. And he really didn't like my plans to use my life and business to help build the Kingdom of God. The problem was, I had no understanding concerning this spiritual war with Satan and therefore, was defenseless. I also had no clue what was going on. At that time in my life, 26 years after becoming a born again Christian, I had never heard a sermon about spiritual warfare and how to defend myself! And in the 30 years since then, I have only heard two or three. Some churches do a better job than others in this area, but as a whole, the Body of Christ is in a state of confusion - decimated and dysfunctional from the schemes of Satan and his forces of darkness. That is why I am writing this book! Every Christian needs to understand how to protect themselves and their family from the forces of darkness and how to *walk in God's power and blessings.* And as I explained in the introduction, this knowledge is critical for those of us who are working in the marketplace.

The Lord began to lead me to people who could teach me about this war. I met a layperson, a very spiritually savvy lady about 70 years old, who I hired to do some transcribing for me. When I went to pick up the typed material, she asked "Bob, what is going on in your life? You have a lot of fear in your voice." I shared some of my story with her. "You are being attacked by Satan," she said, "Do you know anything about spiritual war?" I admitted that I didn't. "You need prayer," she responded. She began to teach me some things about the war with the forces of darkness and she and her friend prayed for me. This encounter birthed my awareness of the common spiritual war that takes place in our minds, something we all experience on a day-to-day basis, but most are dangerously unaware of and unskilled in defending against.

For the last 25 years, I have been on this journey to understand how and why this spiritual war against the forces of darkness works. During this time the Holy Spirit helped me put together truths from Scripture like assembling pieces of a giant jigsaw puzzle. I now understand my real identity as a child of God and how to rely on the power of God in my day-to-day life. I know how to use that knowledge when I'm struggling against the old nature and Satan and his forces of darkness. The foundation of what I learned begins with God's promise to Abraham.

THE COVENANT PROMISE OF GOD, YOUR FATHER IN HEAVEN

The essence of your real identity is founded on The Promise given to Abraham by God the Father. It is an absolute and irrevocable truth! A lot of the confusion in Christianity is largely due to a lack of understanding of kingdom governments and how The Promise affects Christians. To ensure your effectiveness in this spiritual war as a believer in Christ, you must first **fully** understand who you really are under the Covenant Promise of God, your Father in Heaven!

In 1993, I went to Israel on business with my wife. We took advantage of every possible opportunity to visit many places we had read about in the Bible for years. We had a wonderful time experiencing the Bible come to life as we took a tour of Jerusalem, visited the old city of David, walked on paths that Jesus walked, went to the Mount of Olives, visited the Sea of Galilee, etc. During our visit to the Sea of Galilee, we went to a Christian bookstore called *The Galilee Experience.* They were showing a 30 minute video on the history of the Galilee area so we decided to stay and watch it. Despite hearing many people say that visiting Israel is a very spiritual experience, I was not expecting what happened.

The video went into a history of Abraham during which they discussed The Promise God made to bless him and his descendants for his obedience. Immediately, the Lord spoke to me in my mind saying, "That promise was made to you..." I was shocked! First, because of the very clear and specific communication from God - and second, because up to that point in my life I had been taught to believe that The Promise was made only to the Jewish people. When we got back to the hotel that night, I looked up Scriptures concerning The Promise and followed it through a chain of references in the Bible. I was amazed and shocked at what I discovered.

First, let's look at The Promise made to Abraham: *The angel of the LORD called to Abraham from heaven a second time and said, 'I swear by Myself, declares the LORD, that because you have done this and have not withheld your son, your only son, I will surely bless you and make your descendants as numerous as the stars in the sky and as the sand on the seashore. Your descendants will take possession of the cities of their enemies and through your offspring all nations on earth will be blessed, because you have obeyed Me'* (Genesis 22:15-18).

If you are a Gentile believer in Jesus Christ as I am, you may be wondering what The Promise to Abraham has to do with you. The Promise was made to Abraham and his descendants. So who are Abraham's descendants?

A. Of course, the Jewish people are his descendants, *But God said to him, 'Do not be so distressed about the boy and your slave woman. Listen to whatever Sarah tells you, because it is through Isaac that your offspring will be reckoned* (Genesis 21:12). The Jewish people are direct blood descendants of Isaac.

B. Additionally, those who put their trust in Jesus Christ as their Savior and Lord are also his descendants, *For not all who are descended from Israel are Israel. Nor because they are his descendants are they all Abraham's children. On the contrary, 'It is through Isaac that your offspring will be reckoned,'* (referring to Genesis 21:12). *In other words, it is not the children by physical descent who are God's children, but* ***it is the children of the promise who are regarded as Abraham's offspring*** (Romans 9:6-8).

Did you hear that? Paul flat out calls believers in Christ "children of the promise"! He further verifies this in Galatians: *So in Christ Jesus you are all children of God through faith, for all of you who were baptized into Christ have clothed yourselves with Christ. There is neither Jew nor Gentile, neither slave nor free, nor is there male and female, for you are all one in Christ Jesus.* ***If you belong to Christ, then you are Abraham's seed, and heirs according to the promise*** (Galatians 3:26-29).

And again in Ephesians: ***This mystery is that through the gospel the Gentiles are heirs together with Israel, members together of one body, and sharers together in the promise*** *in Christ*

Jesus (Ephesians 3:6). If you are a true believer in Jesus Christ, you have been *born again,* (John 3:3), and in doing so, you have become a member of God's family. As such, you are Abraham's seed, and heirs according to the promise. Notice, as God's children, we are not mere citizens of the Kingdom, but heirs with the King Himself!

Let's examine a sample of the blessings that Scripture says are included under this covenant. The first fourteen verses of Deuteronomy 28 give a long list of blessings that **will** come upon you when you obey God, including: being blessed in the city and the country, receiving blessing on your children, your crops, your cattle, your pantry and your kitchen. God also promises to defeat and scatter your enemies and make them fear you. Also, He promises to bless your storehouses, your land and your work. Finally, He promises to make you wealthier, (you will lend but not borrow), intelligent (you will be the head and not the tail) and influential (you will always be at the top, never the bottom). God is not promising that all of His children will be millionaires, or that they will all have the same amount of wealth. He only promises that they will have more wealth from Him if they obey Him, than if they don't.

Some people I talk to seem to believe The Promise does not apply to the New Covenant of Salvation through faith in Christ. However, the Apostle Paul directly links the New Covenant with The Promise in Roman's 10:5-13. Not to mention the fact that those who put their faith in Christ are Abraham's heirs!

Others try to discredit it by the differences of how God blesses, trains and disciplines each of us and the differences in His plans for each of our lives. Such differences should not be used as evidence or facts to discredit His Promise. If one is going to disregard some of God's promises just because they don't understand or agree with them, then of what value or believability are His other promises to the Body of Christ?

Still others I talk to ask, "What about all the people, Christians included, who don't obey God and have a lot of money?" There could be many reasons for this, including that they understand business science better or manage their money more wisely. But also remember that the earth is currently Satan's dominion and he is as capable of giving people wealth and power as God is. See the temptation of Jesus in Luke 4:4-13.

Scripture also declares that protection will be provided to those who love and obey God. Such promises are also included in the book of Deuteronomy and in Psalm 91.

> *Whoever dwells in the shelter of the Most High will rest in the shadow of the Almighty. I will say of the Lord, "He is my refuge and my fortress, my God, in whom I trust." "Because he loves Me," says the Lord, "I will rescue him; I will protect him, for he acknowledges My name. He will call on Me, and I will answer him; I will be with him in trouble, I will deliver him and honor him. With long life I will satisfy him and show him my salvation" (Psalm 91:1-2 and 14-16).*

Most interesting is the final line where God says, "I will… show him My salvation." The Hebrew word for salvation is Yeshua – which is Jesus' name in Hebrew. All this protection and blessing through Jesus! Do you love and obey Him? I will explain later in this book how you can know.

THE KINGDOM CULTURE

To understand the Kingdom Culture, it is very important to know that under a kingdom government the word of the king is law and, as such, cannot be challenged by its citizens. All creatures in the kingdom, including the king, are bound by the king's word. Therefore, The Promise is the sworn Word of God and since God cannot lie, it is an absolute and irrevocable covenant between God, Abraham and his descendants! *When God made His promise to Abraham, since there was no one greater for Him to swear by, He swore by Himself, saying, 'I will surely bless you and give you many descendants.' ...Because God wanted to make the unchanging nature of His purpose very clear to the heirs of what was promised, He confirmed it with an oath. God did this so that, by two unchangeable things in which it is impossible for God to lie, we who have fled to take hold of the hope offered to us may be greatly encouraged. We have this hope as an anchor for the soul, firm and secure* (Hebrews 6:13-19).

The late Dr. Vernon Grounds, former President of the Denver Seminary, has been a major spiritual influence in my spiritual growth. In one of his books, he noted that the Bible contains equally valid truths that appear to contradict each other. He also noted that many Christians struggle with reconciling these seeming contradictions. It has been my observation that Christian denominations are sometimes built on one side of these equally valid truths in an effort to make people's lives less complicated. These seemingly offsetting truths are the cause of many arguments and contradictions in Christianity.

I have learned while consulting with businesses that the same thing happens in the business world. Frequently, arguments take place because a person has not yet developed wisdom or judgment about when or how to apply such offsetting truths.

For example, in the Bible, we encounter such principles of truth as "grace" versus "works." The Apostle Paul says we are saved by grace. But the Apostle John, in his first epistle, instructs us that we should examine our behavior and works to determine if we are demonstrating that God is really living in us. James even tells us in chapter 2, that faith without deeds is dead. Both of these principles of truth are equally valid.

An example of a seeming contradiction of equally valid truths in the business world is, "You have to spend money to make money" versus "A penny saved is a penny earned." Which of these is true? They both are, you say. The wise person knows that there is a time for everything, as Solomon says in Ecclesiastes. There is a time to "spend money to make money" and a time to not spend money, for the purpose of increasing net profit. There is a time to apply each principle. Wisdom is knowing what time it is!

In the area of supernatural blessings and protection, let me point out that there is more than one spiritual principle of truth at work. In Hannah Whitehall Smith's book *The Christian's Secret of a Happy Life,* she teaches that a Christian will never be happy until he/she accepts the absolute sovereignty of God. For example, even if a person obeys God, He sometimes removes that protection to test him/her as He did with Job. God has this absolute right as our Creator which He points out to Job with great candor. Only He has complete understanding of the circumstances, our heart and motives and the wisdom in such matters to know "what time it is." Our role is to trust Him.

THE KINGDOM OF GOD GOVERNMENT

God's Kingdom government on earth is supernatural (it is invisible and therefore we can't see it at work). What does it mean that the King will use His supernatural power to bless and protect you? First of all, God is an accessible King. He is personally involved in your life. In fact, I would presume that most Christians greatly underestimate just how much He is involved in their lives! In one of his Bible studies, Dr. Bob Beltz said that, "Most Christians think their problems are too big and God is too small." The Scriptures help us see that God is not limited by worldly or natural circumstances. Nothing is impossible for God!

If you settle in a foreign land, and you want the benefits and privileges of the citizenry, you must assimilate yourself into the culture and comply with the rules of the land. Likewise, if you want protection and blessings in the Kingdom of God, by His supernatural power, you must understand Kingdom culture, laws, statutes and rules and comply with them. The same principle of truth applies to corporate cultures. If you go to work in a new job for a different company, you are told, in so many words, that you must do things "their way" if you want to be successful. If you are the leader of that business, you are the one telling them that with your words and actions. A culture, any culture, defines "the way we do things." Nations, governments, companies, and families all have cultures. A culture is comprised of the rules, values, traditions and behavior expected. The Kingdom of God, a theocracy, has a culture also. Listen to the following statements of its King:

> *All authority in Heaven and on Earth has been given to Me* (Matthew 28:18).
>
> *Seek first His kingdom and His righteousness, and all these things will be given to you as well* (Matthew 6:33).
>
> *Jesus said, 'If you hold to My teaching, you are really My disciples. Then you will know the truth, and the truth will set you free'* (John 8:31-32).
>
> *Jesus replied, 'Anyone who loves Me will obey My teaching. My Father will love them, and We will come to them and make Our home with them. Anyone who does not love Me*

will not obey My teaching. These words you hear are not My own; they belong to the Father who sent Me. All this I have spoken while still with you. But the Advocate, the Holy Spirit, Whom the Father will send in My name, will teach you all things and will remind you of everything I have said to you' (John 14:23-26).

So in everything, do to others what you would have them do to you, for this sums up the Law and the Prophets (Matthew 7:12).

The Kingdom of Heaven is like treasure hidden in a field. When a man found it, he hid it again, and then in his joy went and sold all he had and bought that field (Matthew 13:44)

Very truly I tell you, whoever believes in Me will do the works I have been doing, and they will do even greater things than these, because I am going to the Father. And I will do whatever you ask in My name, so that the Father may be glorified in the Son. You may ask Me for anything in My name, and I will do it (John 14:12-14).

How does He know if you believe in Him? Jesus replied, 'Anyone who loves Me will obey My teaching' (John 14:23).

Before we close this chapter, let's look at an example of someone who lived their whole life under the blessing and protection of God. In Genesis 31, we see an example of God's supernatural power and intervention in the economic realm at work to protect and bless Jacob. Let's examine this amazing chain of events:

Jacob heard that Laban's sons were saying, "Jacob has taken

> *everything our father owned and has gained all this wealth from what belonged to our father." And Jacob noticed that Laban's attitude toward him was not what it had been. Then the LORD said to Jacob, "Go back to the land of your fathers and to your relatives, and* ***I will be with you.****" So Jacob sent word to Rachel and Leah to come out to the fields where his flocks were. He said to them, "I see that your father's attitude toward me is not what it was before, but the God of my father has been with me. You know that I've worked for your father with all my strength, yet your father has cheated me by changing my wages ten times. However, God has not allowed him to harm me. If he said, 'The speckled ones will be your wages,' then all the flocks gave birth to speckled young; and if he said, 'The streaked ones will be your wages,' then all the flocks bore streaked young. So God has taken away your father's livestock and has given them to me"* (Genesis 31:1-9).

Notice that, because Laban had been cheating Jacob, God supernaturally intervened, causing all of the livestock to appear as the livestock which Laban had promised to Jacob to fulfill his commitment, thereby enabling Jacob to become wealthy and causing Laban to become poor.

God was with Jacob; He intervened in his life, showed him favor because he had faith in God and trusted The Promise. Because of his faith and obedience, God was with him, He protected and blessed Jacob. From this we learn that God, when He is with you, intervenes in your life to protect and provide for you. In like manner, God intervenes in the midst of your spiritual war, whether Satan is attacking you head on, or by influencing someone in your life in a negative way. When "stuff happens," you have to remember who you are and continually trust and obey God so He is with you. Do this no matter what. Satan is a master of deceptions and lies. Everything he tells you will be a lie or a distortion of the truth.

Remember who you are. You are the Children of God, the Father Almighty! He is YOUR Father! *If God is for us, who can be against us* (Romans 8:31)?

PUT ON THE FULL ARMOR OF GOD FOR PROTECTION!

It doesn't matter if Satan's attacks against you are direct or indirect, you can draw on the power of God to help and protect you. How? By putting on the **full** armor of God! To draw upon the power of God to defeat Satan and his forces of darkness, the Apostle Paul instructs Christians to put on the full armor of God, *so...you may be able to stand your ground, and after you have done everything, to stand. Stand firm...* (From Ephesians 6:11-14).

What is the full armor of God? It is a powerful metaphor of how to walk in the Spirit, use Scriptural truth and draw upon God's divine power to stand against Satan's schemes to keep you out of fellowship with God, block your blessings, ruin you and your career or business and stop you from helping to build God's Kingdom on earth.

BECAUSE GOD WANTED TO MAKE

THE UNCHANGING NATURE OF HIS PURPOSE

VERY CLEAR TO THE HEIRS OF WHAT WAS PROMISED,
HE CONFIRMED IT WITH AN OATH.

GOD DID THIS SO THAT,

BY TWO UNCHANGEABLE THINGS

IN WHICH IT IS IMPOSSIBLE FOR GOD TO LIE,

WE WHO HAVE FLED TO TAKE HOLD OF

THE HOPE SET BEFORE US

MAY BE GREATLY ENCOURAGED.

WE HAVE THIS HOPE AS AN ANCHOR FOR THE SOUL,

FIRM AND SECURE.

Hebrews 6:17-19

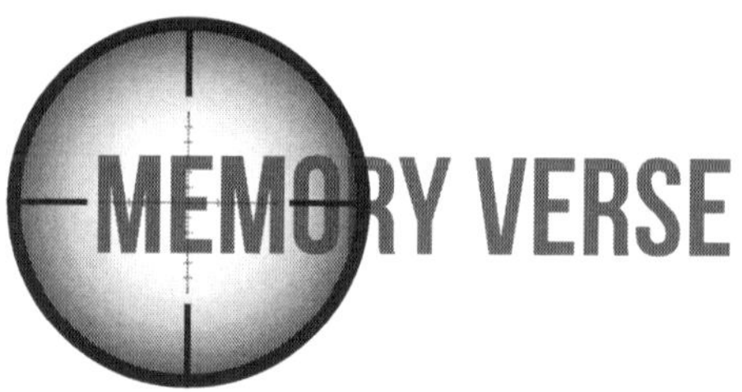

If you belong to Christ, then you are Abraham's seed, and heirs according to the promise.

Galatians 3:29

QUESTIONS FOR CONSIDERATION:

- Up until now, what have you seen your identity to be? What do you see as your identity now?

- According to the Bible, what is your identity in Christ? Why is it important to know that?

- How difficult is it to see yourself each day as God sees you? How are you going to improve this perception?

- How will knowing who you really are help you in business?

- How will knowing who you really are help you win the battle with the spiritual forces of evil?

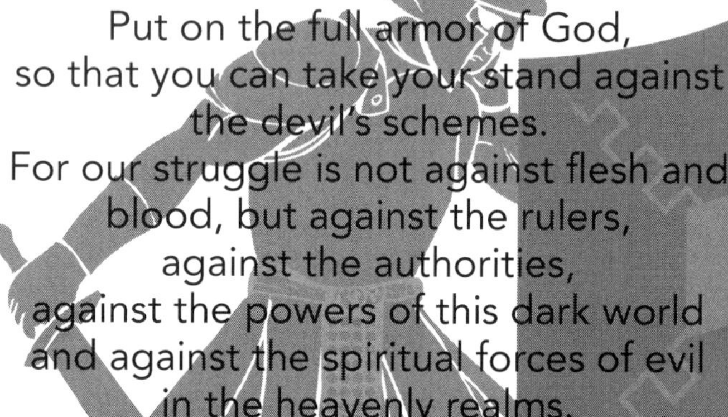

Put on the full armor of God,
so that you can take your stand against
the devil's schemes.
For our struggle is not against flesh and
blood, but against the rulers,
against the authorities,
against the powers of this dark world
and against the spiritual forces of evil
in the heavenly realms.

Ephesians 6:11-12

CHAPTER 3

WHAT YOU NEED TO KNOW ABOUT SATAN AND HIS SCHEMES

It would be an understatement to say that I used to be naïve concerning the cosmic war between God and Satan and his forces of darkness (spiritual warfare). I am convinced that, for the first twenty eight years of my Christian life, I thought of Satan as nothing more than a story book character. Most Christians seem to be unaware and equally naïve of the reality that when they became a Christian they changed sides in this cosmic war, moving from Satan's side (the enemy) to God's side (the body of Christ). Paul describes it this way, *For you were once darkness, but now you are light in the Lord* (Ephesians 5:8).

I would bet money that most of you believe that every thought in your mind comes from your brain. However, in John 10:3-5, the Lord Jesus Christ makes us aware that some of our thoughts come from the spirit realm: *He* (Jesus Christ) *calls His own sheep by name... and His sheep follow Him because they know His voice. But they will never follow a stranger* (Satan); *in fact, they will run away from him because they do not recognize a stranger's voice.* The fact is that both Jesus Christ (through the Spirit of God) and Satan (through his forces of darkness) are communicating with you in your mind. Sound weird again? Not so much. If we, as mere humans, can communicate through wireless radio waves and cell phones, why is it unthinkable that God or Satan can communicate with us through our thoughts? Jesus makes it clear that both He and Satan are communicating with us in our mind.

Satan can plant thoughts in your mind in such a way that you may not even be able to discern their origin. A friend of mine's husband – a highly educated professional - learned this the hard way. The husband, a good man, had been very successful in the investment industry. In a moment of weakness, he got an idea in his mind for a way to make more money. The enemy provided rationalization that legally it was a gray area and therefore not illegal. The thought of making more money appealed to "the flesh." He followed through and was later convicted of a felony. He is now serving time in prison, his reputation destroyed by the enemy and their life is in shambles. Thankfully his wife is sticking by his side, both of them working through this, looking forward to the time that they can begin rebuilding their lives.

If you are to be victorious in this war and overcome Satan, you are going to need knowledge. Knowledge concerning the enemy, knowledge of your Kingdom resources available to fight the enemy and understanding of how to use them! Whether they know it or not, all of mankind is engaged in three separate struggles with: 1) The World; 2) The Flesh; and 3) Satan. Many Christians are unfamiliar with these teachings, making them easy prey for Satan to have his way in their lives.

When experienced businesses owners want to improve

their strength, profit and growth, emerging from the rivalry with their competitors as industry leaders, they study the strategies of their competitors and analyze the industry forces impacting their company's ability to grow and thrive. Once they understand the impact of those industry forces they can develop a formal strategic plan to outwit the competition.

In like manner, if you want to overcome the forces of darkness and defeat them, you must first understand their schemes and be prepared to defend yourself against their attacks. These schemes are designed to keep you from experiencing the full life Jesus wants for you and to stop you from participating in the advancement of the Kingdom of God on earth. I have studied Satan's schemes extensively. This chapter and the following eight chapters are designed to educate you and prepare you to win this spiritual warfare with the forces of darkness. This is not my plan, it is the plan laid out throughout Scripture.

AS A MEMBER OF GOD'S FAMILY, SATAN IS AT WAR WITH YOU

A friend and business owner once told me, "I would like to have a Bible study in my business, but I don't know if I can deal with the spiritual war with Satan." It is true, the more serious we are about helping Christ build his Church, the more Satan will battle against us. But he can't win if we learn to stand *firm* with the *Armor of God* on.

Pastor Shafer Parker Jr. of Hawkwood Baptist Fellowship says, "When you believed in Jesus, you received eternal life. Your sins were forgiven. God became your Father in the fullest sense of the term. Heaven became your home and your ultimate destination. The Holy Spirit of God took up residence in your heart and became your ever-present Companion (and Counselor). The people of God became your forever family, along with God the Father and Christ the Son... But along with those benefits, you also got noticed by the enemy. You see, if you belong to Jesus, the devil hates you and singles you out for his particular attention. When a man or woman is truly born again, Satan knows he can never have that soul. But he also knows that the best way to preserve the souls he still has is to make certain that as many Christians as possible remain as ineffective as possible."

As discussed in Chapter 1, when you believe Jesus Christ is the Son of God, and you invite Him into your life to rescue you from your sinful nature, forgive you for sinning, and ask Him to be the Lord of your life, you are born again. That is, you are literally born into God's family. Prior to becoming a child of God, Satan and his forces of evil were trying to stop you from believing in Christ by making you question the need for Him, stop you from believing in Him, and/or stop you from putting your trust in Him. But the moment you become a child of God, Satan and the forces of evil are trying to keep you from obeying Him, keep you from maturing (growing up) spiritually, and keep you from working at building the Kingdom of God on earth (referred to in Christianity as The Great Commission).

In his online sermons, Pastor Parker reminds Christians "that we believe in a personal God. That is, we believe God can be known in the same way we know one another. He hears us when we pray and He cares about what we have to say. He thinks of us individually and has plans for each one of us." [1]

Then Pastor Parker discusses one of the most profound insights into reality I have ever encountered: "The Bible also teaches that a personality lies behind the evil in this world. The devil is as real as

---

1 See Psalm 139:13-16 and Isaiah 41:9-13 to support his comments.

God, although he is not the same as God…he, like us and like all the angels, is a created being, dependent on God for his continued existence. But for all that, never forget he is also a personal being. He communicates with us, after a fashion…he can develop special strategies for individuals. There are people in which he takes special interest. And he is constantly seeking out those whom he can devour, metaphorically speaking." [2]

My observation after being a Christian since 1957 is that most Christians treat Satan just as I used to - a fairy tale character, not a real being that has been, is now and will continue to be personally interacting in their lives on earth. His objectives are to *steal, kill, and destroy.* As I look back over my life, I now see how Satan has used a series of strategies throughout my entire life to keep me from becoming a child of God, derail my spiritual growth after I became His child, create disruptions and undermine my desire to help build the Kingdom of God. I suspect that you will see the same thing, if you review your life as well.

Satan hates God and is at war with Him. The children of God collectively (referred to in the Bible as the "Body of Christ") are God's presence on earth. Therefore, it stands to reason that if you are a member of God's family, Satan is at war with you! Why? Because the Body of Christ is God's physical presence on earth! The Lord Jesus Christ makes this sobering reality clear, *The thief* (the devil) *comes only to steal and kill and destroy* (John 10:10). But, in Ephesians 6, the Bible teaches that God's children can *be strong in the Lord and in His mighty power by putting on the full armor of God so that you can take your stand against the devil's schemes.*

---

2 See John 10, Ephesians 6:10-16, and 1 Peter 5:8-11 for further study.

USING GOD'S STRENGTH TO STAND AGAINST SATAN!

There are three key reasons you need to "be strong in the Lord and in His mighty power."

1. **We need God's strength to achieve His objectives.** His objectives include our spiritual growth, the outcome of which is summarized in Galatians 5:22-26, His Great Commission in Matthew 28:18-20, and His plan for our lives, see Jeremiah 29:11 and Psalm 139:13-16.
2. **We need God's strength to regularly defend ourselves against Satan.** This includes both external attacks and internal attacks – External, because Satan would have us believe our battle is against people (Ephesians 6:12); and Internal, summarized in the temptation of Jesus in Luke 4:1-13. Also see Satan's Strategies below.
3. **We need God's strength when Satan comes at us with all he's got!** 1 Peter 5:8-11 says, *Your enemy the devil prowls around like a roaring lion looking for someone to devour. Resist him, standing firm in the faith, because you know that your brothers throughout the world are undergoing the same kind of suffering.*

Why do we need strength to defend ourselves against Satan? Because, apart from the power of God's weapons, Satan is much too powerful for us to defeat! As the ruler of this world and *the god of this age* (2 Corinthians 4:4), Satan is extremely capable of tricking, pressuring and manipulating us into distrusting God, becoming a slave to the sinful nature and conforming us to the plan he has for our eternal separation from God.

WE NEED GOD'S STRENGTH:

- To accomplish His objectives, including the Great Commission.
- To attain the fruit of the Spirit character qualities outlined in Galatians 5, love, joy, peace, patience, kindness, goodness, faithfulness, gentleness and self-control.
- To resist Satan's external attacks such as peer pressure, need for approval and acceptance, threats on our life, need for employment, need for family, being politically correct, the confusion of good and evil by world authorities and "intellectuals," etc. The devil's list of schemes to derail our spiritual growth and the advancement of the Kingdom on earth seems almost endless. Be alert!
- To defend against Satan's internal attacks against the mind, James 4:7.
- To do good works, Ephesians 2:10
- For God to glorify Himself through us, Ephesians 3:10.
- To stand in grace, Ephesians 3:12.

The Apostle Paul makes it very clear that our battle is not against humans. Nonetheless, it is humans we always tend to blame or get frustrated and angry with. We do this in spite of the fact that Christ commands us in John 15:12 to *Love each other as I have loved you.* Then He promises us access to His power if we obey Him, *If you remain in Me and My words remain in you, ask whatever you wish, and it will be done for you* (v.7).

How do we love each other as Christ loved us? Paul defines it for us in 1 Corinthians 13, *Love is patient, love is kind. It does not envy, it does not boast, it does not dishonor others. It is not rude, it is not self-seeking, it is not easily angered, it keeps no record of wrongs. Love does not delight in evil but rejoices with the truth. It always protects, always trusts, always hopes, always perseveres.*

Of course the devil likes it when we war against each other – nations, families, churches, husbands/wives, parents/children, males/females, races, friends, etc. Satan wants to destroy any form of relationship that is a threat to his plans and survival. In addition, our disobedience to Christ distances us from His power.

Satan and his forces of darkness are very powerful (by our standards) and can't be defeated by methods used to war against humans. This can be a very difficult lesson for business leaders and managers to learn because they are accustomed to overcoming opposition and obstacles to accomplish results by using their own intelligence, talents and strength. However, the Bible teaches us that the war against the forces of evil requires spiritual weapons containing the power of God to defeat Satan and his forces of darkness, *The weapons we fight with are not the weapons of the world. On the contrary, they have divine power to demolish strongholds. We demolish arguments and every pretension that sets itself up against the knowledge of God, and we take captive every thought to make it obedient to Christ* (2 Corinthians 10:4-5).

SATAN HAS STRATEGIES TO KEEP YOU FROM GROWING AND BUILDING THE KINGDOM

As a strategic business planner, I was intrigued by Paul's statement that Satan has strategies. After studying his strategies and looking back over my life, I can see where he has used them to make me ineffective and disobedient at times. It has been one of my missions in life to discover his strategies and expose them to the Body of Christ. The devil has several schemes that he employs. Based on my research, following are Satan's core strategies:

- **He lies to you by questioning God's truth** (Genesis 3:1).

- **He lies (sometimes mixing lies with truth, if necessary) to persuade you to disobey God** (Genesis 3:4-7).
- **He manipulates you until your love for seeking the desires of your heart is greater than your love for seeking God** (Matthew 22:37).
- **He exploits your weaknesses** by tempting you with the lust of the flesh, the lust of the eyes, and the pride of life (1 John 2:16).
- **He uses a divide and conquer strategy.** He gets you battling people instead of him and the spiritual forces of darkness (Ephesians 6:12).

Consider how the devil tempted Christ, even using Scripture to try to manipulate Him:

Jesus, full of the Holy Spirit, left the Jordan and was led by the Spirit into the wilderness, where for forty days He was tempted by the devil. He ate nothing during those days, and at the end of them He was hungry. The devil said to Him, "If you are the Son of God, tell this stone to become bread." Jesus answered, "It is written: 'Man shall not live on bread alone.'" The devil led Him up to a high place and showed Him in an instant all the kingdoms of the world. And he said to Him, "I will give you all their authority and splendor; it has been given to me, and I can give it to anyone I want to. If You worship me, it will all be Yours." Jesus answered, "It is written: 'Worship the Lord your God and serve Him only.'" The devil led Him to Jerusalem and had Him stand on the highest point of the temple. "If You are the Son of God," he said, "throw Yourself down from here. For it is written: "'He will command His angels concerning you to guard you carefully; they will lift you up in their hands, so that you will not strike your foot against a stone.'" Jesus answered, "It is said: 'Do not put the Lord your God to the test.'" When the devil had finished all this tempting, he left Him until an opportune time (Luke 4:1-13).

Note that the devil even used Scripture to try to trick Christ. And note that Christ **always** used the Word of God (a Spiritual Weapon) to defend Himself against the devil's temptations.

All spiritual battles begin in your mind. Paul tells us in Colossians to *Set your minds on things above, not on earthly things* (Colossians 3:2). Both God and Satan desire to influence your mind. The challenge for you is to discern which voice to listen to. Then believe and trust the Word of God with your choices and actions, instead of Satan's lies and temptations.

As a business person, owner or professional, Satan desires to ruin your life and career to minimize or eliminate your effectiveness in helping to build the Kingdom of God. He will attempt to:

- Minimize your knowledge, wisdom and understanding of powerful spiritual and business secrets.
- Destroy your reputation and integrity.
- Diminish the flow of your supernatural blessings and protection from God.

Some of the key schemes he will use to accomplish these objectives are:

- **He lies, making his lies appear to be reality.** *He* (Satan) *was a murderer from the beginning, not holding to the truth, for there is no truth in him. When he lies, he speaks his native language, for he is a liar and the father of lies* (John 8:44). *Satan himself masquerades as an angel of light* (2 Corinthians 11:14).
- **He wants you to disobey God.** ALL of God's blessings and rewards are tied to obedience: *Anyone who loves Me will obey My teaching. My Father will love them, and We will come to them and make Our home with them* (John 14:23). Deuteronomy 28:2, *All these blessings will come upon you and accompany you if you obey the Lord your God.* There are many other promises in Scripture that result

from our obedience. See Genesis 2:15-17, Deuteronomy 6-8, 28 and 30, Psalm 1 and John 14:21, and 15:10.

- **He lies about God,** leading people to believe there are gods that are equal to Him in power and/or authority. There is only one God: *Hear, O Israel: the Lord our God, the Lord is One* (Deuteronomy 6:4). And He does not share power: *You shall have no other gods before Me* (Exodus 20:3). *For there is one God and one mediator between God and mankind, the man Christ Jesus* (1 Timothy 2:5).
- **He lies about the path to God,** leading people to believe there are multiple ways to be united in fellowship with God. However, the Bible makes it clear there is only one path to God as seen in 1 Timothy 2:5 above and Jesus speaking in John 14:6 *I am the way and the truth and the life. No one comes to the Father except through Me.*
- **He mixes truth and lies to confuse, manipulate and tempt you** as he did in the beginning with Eve in Genesis 3:4-5 *You will not certainly die…For God knows that when you eat from it your eyes will be opened, and you will be like God, knowing good and evil.* As it turns out, Adam and Eve's eyes were opened (God knew this was not good for them). But, Adam and Eve did die – both physically and spiritually, creating the monumental problem for mankind discussed in Chapter 1.
- **He uses accusations,** creating false guilt to keep us down. A clue to one of his schemes is his name, *Satan,* which means adversary or *diabolos* (translated devil), which means accuser. Of course if he fails at that, he will lie about us to keep us down.
- **He will battle to keep the souls of non-Christians** by making them feel like they are not "good enough" yet to come to God. He uses lies about God so people will distrust Him and he manipulates people to put off inviting Christ into their lives. By using these strategies, he starts people on a fruitless mission (because a person

can only become "good enough" through the power of God's Spirit in them, which only happens once they put their faith in Christ and invite Him into their life).

- **He will make Christians feel inadequate** or like a failure in their Christian walk, discouraging them from growing spiritually and/or diminishing or eliminating their Kingdom effectiveness:
  - Satan does his best to find something he can make us feel guilty about because he knows a Christian who feels guilty is discouraged and ineffective.
  - Satan uses accusations to destroy relationships, trust and unity in families, The Church - the Body of Christ or any other group of Christians trying to work together.
  - Satan will jump at any opportunity from our slip-ups to convince us to focus on our guilt instead of Christ's redeeming work of grace at the cross.
- **Unless we keep our eyes on Jesus every day, Satan will lead us astray** for as long as it takes for us to:
  - Believe we can sin without consequences because of God's grace; and/or
  - Become a slave to the "sinful nature" again.
- **Satan uses fear to manipulate us.** *For God has not given us a spirit of fear, but of power and of love and of a sound mind* (2 Timothy 1:7 NKJV). **Or to destroy us!** *But we do not belong to those who shrink back and are destroyed, but to those who have faith and are saved* (Hebrews 10:39). Thankfully, God loves us. *God is love. Whoever lives in love lives in God, and God in them. This is how love is made complete among us so that we will have confidence on the day of judgment: In this world we are like Jesus. There is no fear in love. But perfect love drives out fear, because fear has to do with punishment. The one who fears is not made perfect in love* (1 John 4:16-18).
- **His most powerful strategy is to try to overwhelm**

you by appealing to the flesh. *Simon, Simon, Satan has asked to sift all of you as wheat. But I have prayed for you, Simon, that your faith may not fail* (Luke 22:31-32). Satan will use "flaming arrows" with temptations to attack your infirmities (weaknesses in the flesh), such as addictions of all kinds including alcohol, drugs, food, tobacco, sex, homosexuality, money, people, things, activity, power, etc.

- **Satan will use rationalization to move you out from under the protection of God** by disobeying Him. For example, Christ commanded Christians to love one another. Yet, they violate the principles of Psalm 15 daily. *Lord, who may dwell in Your sacred tent? Who may live on Your holy mountain? The one whose walk is blameless, who does what is righteous, who speaks the truth from their heart; whose tongue utters no slander, who does no wrong to a neighbor, and casts no slur on others; who despises a vile person but honors those who fear the Lord; who keeps an oath even when it hurts, and does not change their mind; who lends money to the poor without interest; who does not accept a bribe against the innocent. Whoever does these things will never be shaken.*
- **He will get you in a busyness trap from the worries of this world and/or making money.** *Still others, like seed sown among thorns, hear the word; but the worries of this life, the deceitfulness of wealth and the desires for other things come in and choke the word, making it unfruitful* (Mark 4:13-20).
- **One of Satan's most effective strategies is discouragement.** For those who might be thinking that I am over-concentrating on Satan and His impact on the lives of Christians, consider these shocking statistics from research distilled by *Schaeffer Institute* from their own research and that of *Barna, Focus on the Family,* and *Fuller Seminary:*
    - Fifteen hundred pastors leave the ministry each month due to moral failure, spiritual burnout, or

contention in their churches.

- Fifty percent of pastors' marriages will end in divorce.
- Eighty percent of pastors feel unqualified and discouraged in their role as pastor.
- Fifty percent of pastors are so discouraged that they would leave the ministry if they could, but have no other way of making a living.
- Eighty percent of seminary and Bible school graduates who enter the ministry will leave the ministry within the first five years.
- Seventy percent of pastors constantly fight depression.
- Almost forty percent polled said they have had an extra-marital affair since beginning their ministry.
- Seventy percent said the only time they spend studying the Word is when they are preparing their sermons. [3]

It appears from this study that seminary-trained pastors, taken as a whole, are as naive and unequipped in coping with Satan and his spiritual forces of darkness as those of us sitting in the pews. I think this sufficiently documents my presupposition that the Body of Christ is dysfunctional and in a state of shambles from the schemes of the enemy.

YOU HAVE SPIRITUAL WEAPONS WITH DIVINE POWER TO DEFEAT SATAN

One of my friends is a marketplace leader in Florida whom God has called to teach Kingdom economics in the marketplace. He has no seminary degree. Like me, he is simply a business man who has a passion to teach people practical applications of Kingdom of God principles in the marketplace. I asked him to share how Satan

3 © 2007 (research from 1989 to 2006) R. J. Krejcir Ph.D. Francis A. Schaeffer Institute of Church Leadership Development

tried to discourage him from continuing his marketplace ministry to the business domain. His story follows:

I was holding a marketplace conference in a south central African nation. I was told there would be 500-1000 in attendance. I had spent 6 weeks preparing my spirit for this event and there was a great sense of expectation. Unfortunately, the planning on the sponsor's end was poor and that nation was playing their arch-rival in soccer on the day of the conference. The entire nation turned out to see this match and we ended up with 100 people in attendance. I delivered the message I had prepared for almost all day Saturday and did it with zeal. When I returned to my hotel room, I had a conversation with the Lord. 'Lord, I'm done! I have failed you, my wife, and these people. You just can't send me all over the world to bring this message of Your economy for 100 people. How am I supposed to change this economy with 100 people? I'm in a foreign country, away from my wife and kids, I've invested thousands of dollars of Your money, and I'm a failure.' I was feeling total despair, hopelessness, and a sense of total failure. I told the Lord I was not going to go all over the world any more. What I did not realize during my despair was that my hotel was a few doors down from the national witchcraft museum, and I was an unwelcome visitor. That was Saturday night and I was leaving on Tuesday at 5 am to fly back to the States.

Monday morning I received a phone call. 'Brother, I was at your conference Saturday and I was overwhelmed by that message. I've never heard anything like that. I am the general manager of a radio station and I would like to interview you on this subject.' This was one of the poorest countries in the world where the average annual income was under $400 per year, so I was not impressed by his general manager status. I pictured his wife turning a generator outside his garage while he was talking on his homemade radio station. I was reluctant, but agreed. We drove out in the African bush and I felt my fears were confirmed. Suddenly, we *were met by a well-dressed guard and entered a beautiful compound where there was a Bible school and state of the art radio station. To my amazement, I found myself delivering the message I had prepared for the last 6 weeks (with fasting, prayer and study) to an audience of hundreds of millions of Africans in every country on the continent except Arabic North Africa. After I delivered those messages on that radio broadcast, the despair and depression left me. They continued to broadcast these messages several times in the month after I returned home. One day I got an email from the general manager. 'We have been absolutely inundated with letters and emails from all over the continent of Africa. We have never had this kind of response to any program we have ever done. They are asking us questions we can't answer. Will you consider doing a weekly radio broadcast for us on the Kingdom Economy?'*

My six weeks of preparation and prayer was certainly for the 100, but unknown to me, it was also for the entire continent of Africa. I have often thought about what would have happened, had I allowed the despair and hopelessness to consume me and had rejected the general manager's request. I believe my life would have taken a different course if I had allowed Satan to convince me to quit.

Currently, my friend is working with the political and business leaders in a developing country, teaching them how to apply Kingdom economics to the development of their nation and businesses.

Some of us are called to share with family, neighbors, business associates or people we work with. Some are called to teach 10, 100, 1000, or even whole nations about the love of Christ. But we are all called by the King to make disciples in some way.

Pastor Shafer Parker discusses some powerful insights into what it means to be found standing when the battles are over:

» **"All battles are spiritual battles.** Moses, Joshua, David,

Jesus - all their battles were won first in the realm of the Spirit.

- **All battles are won or lost on the battlefield of the soul.** From heaven's point of view, instant defeat accompanies any compromise against righteousness, no matter how small.
- **In every battle the real prize is the maintenance of your soul.** *What good will it be for someone to gain the whole world, yet forfeit their soul?* (Matthew 16:26).
- **There is no victory apart from a willingness to be emptied.** How about Job? He was a winner in the cosmic struggle whose battle was won the moment he could say, *Naked I came from my mother's womb, and naked I will depart. The Lord gave and the Lord has taken away; may the name of the Lord be praised* (Job 1:21).
- **All victorious battles are fought by a combination of prayer, faith, scripture and action.** Strategy has little to do with it, unless you are strategizing how best to glorify God. *For the battle is the Lord's, and He will deliver you into our hand* (1 Samuel 17:47b NET).
- **All outcomes are decided by heaven's standards, not earth's.** *For God will bring every deed into judgment, including every hidden thing, whether it is good or evil* (Ecclesiastes 12:14).
- **No winner is finally declared until God releases His ruling on Judgment Day.** *Then I saw a great white throne and Him Who was seated on it. ...And I saw the dead, great and small, standing before the throne, and books were opened. Another book was opened, which is the book of life. The dead were judged according to what they had done as recorded in the books. The sea gave up the dead that were in it, and death and Hades gave up the dead that were in them, and each person was judged according to what they had done. ...Anyone whose name was not found written in the book of life was thrown into the lake of fire* (Revelation 20:11-15).

I know this is "heavy stuff," but ***Do not let your hearts be troubled*** (John 14:1). ***The One who is in you is greater than the one who is in the world*** (1 John 4:4).

Next we will examine our spiritual weapons for this war because, *The weapons we fight with are not the weapons of the world. On the contrary, they have divine power to demolish strongholds. We demolish arguments and every pretension that sets itself up against the knowledge of God, and we take captive every thought to make it obedient to Christ* (2 Corinthians 10:4-5).

You can know how to overcome the enemy's schemes and defeat him if you learn and practice daily how to effectively do battle using the Full Armor of God.

BE STRONG IN THE LORD

AND IN HIS MIGHTY POWER.
PUT ON THE FULL ARMOR OF GOD,
SO THAT YOU CAN TAKE YOUR STAND
AGAINST THE DEVIL'S SCHEMES.
FOR OUR STRUGGLE IS NOT AGAINST FLESH AND BLOOD,
BUT AGAINST THE RULERS,
AGAINST THE AUTHORITIES,
AGAINST THE POWERS OF THIS DARK WORLD
AND AGAINST THE SPIRITUAL FORCES OF EVIL
IN THE HEAVENLY REALMS.
THEREFORE PUT ON THE FULL ARMOR OF GOD,
SO THAT WHEN THE DAY OF EVIL COMES,
YOU MAY BE ABLE TO STAND YOUR GROUND,
AND AFTER YOU HAVE DONE EVERYTHING,
TO STAND.
STAND FIRM THEN,
WITH THE BELT OF TRUTH BUCKLED AROUND YOUR WAIST,
WITH THE BREASTPLATE OF RIGHTEOUSNESS IN PLACE,
AND WITH YOUR FEET FITTED WITH THE READINESS
THAT COMES FROM THE GOSPEL OF PEACE.
IN ADDITION TO ALL THIS, TAKE UP THE SHIELD OF FAITH,
WITH WHICH YOU CAN EXTINGUISH
ALL THE FLAMING ARROWS OF THE EVIL ONE.
TAKE THE HELMET OF SALVATION
AND THE SWORD OF THE SPIRIT,
WHICH IS THE WORD OF GOD.
AND PRAY IN THE SPIRIT ON ALL OCCASIONS
WITH ALL KINDS OF PRAYERS AND REQUESTS.
WITH THIS IN MIND, BE ALERT AND ALWAYS
KEEP ON PRAYING FOR ALL THE LORD'S PEOPLE.

The Apostle Paul

For our struggle is not against flesh and blood, but against the rulers, against the authorities, against the powers of this dark world and against the spiritual forces of evil in the heavenly realms.

Ephesians 6:12

QUESTIONS FOR CONSIDERATION:

- How real is Satan to you? Do you recognize when he is communicating with your mind?
- What is a scheme? What scheme(s) might Satan use to destroy your career or business?
- What are Satan's five core strategies? Which one(s) does he use most in the business domain?
- Why do you need God's power to win the battle with Satan? How can you use it in your career or business?
- Describe one or more strategies that Satan has used or is currently using to derail your spiritual growth, break your fellowship with God or stop your involvement in building the Kingdom of God in your daily life.

Jesus answered,
"You say that I am a king.
In fact, the reason I was born and
came into the world is to testify to the
truth. Everyone on the side of truth
listens to Me."

John 18:37

THE BELT OF TRUTH

CHAPTER 4

THE BELT OF TRUTH

The Bible tells Christians that they can be protected from Satan and even overcome him and the forces of darkness by putting on the full Armor of God because each piece has divine power to demolish strongholds. One of my long-term friends made this observation, "I get dressed every morning to go out into the world. How much more important is it to put on the armor of God before I go?"

To effectively battle Satan, the Apostle Paul instructs Christians to *put on the <u>full</u> armor of God, so…you may be able to stand your ground, and after you have done everything, to stand* (Ephesians 6:13). Spiritual battles take place in your mind. Remember our discussion about discerning the voices that attempt to influence us? *He calls His own sheep by name...and His sheep follow Him because they know His voice. But they will never follow a stranger;* in fact, they *will run away from him because they do not recognize a stranger's voice* (John 10:3-5).

The important question is: Will you believe the Holy Spirit and the word of God or Satan's lies and temptations? The enemy will do whatever he can to manipulate your feelings and decisions, including using others who have learned his lies to teach you so that they influence you to believe his lies. Learning to discern whose voice you are listening to and acting on, is a matter of developing sound judgment through daily awareness and practice.

Putting on the **full** armor of God is critical to our ability to stand firm against the enemy. Let's take a look at this armor, piece by piece.

PUTTING ON THE BELT OF TRUTH

Paul first instructs us to, *Stand firm then, with the belt of truth buckled around your waist.*

"The belt—known as the cingulum or balteus—played a crucial role in the effectiveness of a soldier's armor. It was the belt that held the scabbard, without which there would be no place to put a sword. Imagine an overzealous soldier, fired up and charging out into battle—but without his belt, and consequently without a weapon! In addition, the Nelson Study Bible says from the belt 'hung strips of leather to protect the lower body.' The Matthew Henry Commentary says the belt 'girds on [secures] all the other pieces of our armor.' Truth should cling to us as a belt clings to our body." [1]

Paul begins his instruction of God's armor with the Belt of Truth because Satan's chief weapon is lies. In his book, Leadership is an Art, Max DePree says, "The first responsibility of leadership is to define reality." Before you can take any effective action, you

---

1 This text and some others in this book are from the Bible Study Guides at www.freebiblestudyguides.org. I am indebted to them for this valuable resource.

must first know what the truth (reality) of the situation is. When facing opposition from Satan, you need to know the truth in order to recognize his lies. The word of God agrees that defining reality is your first priority: *For the time will come when people will not put up with sound doctrine. Instead, to suit their own desires, they will gather around them a great number of teachers to say what their itching ears want to hear. They will turn their ears away from the truth and turn aside to myths* (2 Timothy 4:3-4). In the Greek, the word used for truth is *aletheia*, "signifying 'the reality lying at the basis of an appearance; the manifested, veritable (absolute) essence of a matter.'" [2]

Therefore, **the Belt of Truth,** which holds your weapon, the Sword of the Lord, is to be seen as representing reality (the truth behind what we can see) – reality you can believe in, put your trust in, live your life by and make your decisions by. God gave us the Bible - His Word (truth) - and the Holy Spirit - the Spirit of truth - who Christ says will lead us to all truth (John 16:13). He gave the Word to us to lead us safely through the darkness, the maze of lies and deception of the enemy, who the Apostle Paul says *masquerades as an angel of light* (2 Corinthians 11:14). Satan's lies are not only inter-mixed into our Christian lives, but in the entire world. That is why God gave us His word and the Holy Spirit to *lead us to all truth* (reality). The Belt of Truth "girds on [secures] all the other pieces of our armor." Truth is foundational to all the other pieces of our spiritual armor. To know reality and be prepared to make sound decisions at work each day, you must read the Bible and seek counsel from the Holy Spirit.

---

2 Vine's Expository Dictionary of Biblical Words.

SATAN'S SCHEMES AND YOUR PREPAREDNESS

From a spiritual perspective, Paul tells Christians to reject (not receive into our mind or emotions) any thought that will cause us to stumble or fall during our daily battle. The Apostle Peter clarifies this, *Therefore* ***gird up the loins of your mind,*** *be sober, and rest your hope fully upon the grace that is to be brought to you at the revelation of Jesus Christ; as obedient children, not conforming yourselves to the former lusts, as in your ignorance; but as He who called you is holy, you also be holy in all your conduct, because it is written, 'Be holy, for I am holy'* (1 Peter 1:13-16 NKJV).

Satan, in his quest to destroy your career or business, wants to make you believe that exercising self-control over your mind and the old nature is a futile endeavor. I have had many Christians, including some pastors, tell me it is not possible for humans to be holy. Really? Do they believe God would ask us to do something that is impossible? *With God, all things are possible* (Matthew 19:26).

Satan lies or twists the truth about anything that will accomplish his objectives, attempting to make his lies appear as reality. *You belong to your father, the devil, and you want to carry out your father's desires. He was a murderer from the beginning, not holding to the truth, for there is no truth in him. When he lies, he speaks his native language, for he is a liar and the father of lies* (John 8:44). What makes him really dangerous is that *Satan himself masquerades as an angel of light* (2 Corinthians 11:14).

Knowing truth (reality) is the foundation of your battle with Satan. Peter and Paul are telling us to prepare our minds and emotions for battle by putting on the belt of truth, which begins by girding up the loins of your mind by putting God's word in it! There are many ways to put God's word in your mind, including:

1. Memorize passages of Scripture. Even if you can't memorize easily, Jesus says, *the Advocate, the Holy Spirit, whom the Father will send in My* (Jesus) *name, will teach you all things and will remind you of everything I have said to you* (in the Bible or in your mind) (John 14:26).
2. Study the Bible on a regular basis.
3. Meditate on passages of Scripture. *Keep this book of the Law always on your lips: meditate on it day and night* (Joshua 1:8).
4. Hear the Word preached. *Consequently, faith comes from hearing the message...*(Romans 10:17).

There is only one way to prepare your emotions for the oncoming battle, and that is to make a permanent decision to have your mind set on what the Spirit desires, *Those who live according to the flesh have their minds set on what the flesh desires; but those who live in accordance with the Spirit have their minds set on what the Spirit desires. The mind governed by the flesh is death, but the mind governed by the Spirit is life and peace* (Romans 8:5-6).

Paul confirms that we can put off our old self and put on the new self, *created to be like God in true righteousness and holiness* in Ephesians 4. Then he instructs us to: *Be strong in the Lord and in His mighty power, by putting on the full armor of God* in chapter 6. Putting off your old self, putting on your new self and setting your mind on what the Spirit desires is imperative to putting on the *full armor of God* so that you have His protection from Satan!

Pastor Parker says, "Integrity is achieved when you and I are in private what we appear to be in public." Isn't it an impossibly high standard to expect us to be perfect in all our conduct, both private and public? Perhaps it is literally. But not substantially, when you consider that when we confess ourselves to be sinners saved by grace, we take on the righteousness of Christ and His power in us to live the life He has requested of us. Thereafter, when we discover sin in ourselves, we immediately repent and seek forgiveness from the offended one, whether God or man (1 John 1:9). When we learn to live like that – in private or in public - the devil has no opportunity to get a foothold in our lives.

TRUTH CAN BE DIVIDED INTO FOUR TYPES

In dealing with the spiritual forces of darkness, we need to know truth. Truth can be broken down into the following four types:

1. **Foundational truth - Reality.** The truth about God, His character, His Kingdom, His power, His promises, His Commands and the way He made things to work in His creation and culture. There is only one God and He says, *You shall have no other gods before Me* (Exodus 20:3). He is totally trustworthy and if you obey Him, you will receive what He promises (Deuteronomy 28-30 and John 14 & 15). This is very important to remember in business, especially for business leaders, managers and advisers. Why? Because "the first responsibility of leadership is to define reality."
2. **Truth about Jesus and His teaching.** He is the only begotten Son of God, the Messiah, the only way to enter God's Kingdom, the High Priest in God's Temple, King of God's Kingdom, the head of the Body of Christ and the one mediator between God and man. *For there is one God and one mediator between God and mankind, the man Christ Jesus, who gave Himself as a ransom for all people* (1 Timothy 2:5-6).
3. **The truth about you.** You are made in God's image, you can be renewed back to man's original nature (Ephesians 4:24) and if you are a Real Christian, *you are a chosen people, a royal priesthood, a holy nation, God's special possession…* (1 Peter 2:9). Did you hear what Peter is saying? God's children are royalty - chosen by God the Father Himself! You are the body of Christ, a

"holy nation" on earth, a people belonging to God and citizens of His Kingdom. *See what great love the Father has lavished on us, that we should be called children of God! And that is what we are* (1 John 3:1)!

4. **Truth in your inner-most being.** It takes truth in your inward parts to cooperate with the renewing of your mind, a work of the Spirit of God, your Counselor and the Spirit of truth. The enemy has schemes to deceive you about yourself and reality. The best way to outwit him is to cultivate a high level of integrity and honesty regarding yourself in your mind and in your soul. *Yet You desired faithfulness even in the womb; You taught me wisdom in that secret place* (Psalm 51:6). Pastor Parker says, "Hypocrisy does not mean saying one thing and doing the opposite. It means saying something that one does not believe. Take the example of getting drunk. Let's say that someone believes that getting drunk is immoral. Does it make that man a hypocrite if he gets drunk? No, it makes him weak…A hypocrite, on the other hand, is someone who might say, 'it's okay for me to get drunk, but not for you.'"

So how does one learn fundamental truth - the truth about God, his Son Jesus and His teachings, the truth about you, and the truth in your inward parts? Read the Bible, pray, go to a church that preaches from the Bible, ask the Holy Spirit to lead you to the truth and apply the word of God in your life daily, *If you love me, keep My commands. And I will ask the Father, and He will give you another Advocate to help you and be with you forever— the Spirit of truth. The Advocate, the Holy Spirit, Whom the Father will send in My name, will teach you all things and will remind you of everything I have said to you. I have much more to say to you, more than you can now bear. But when He, the Spirit of truth, comes, He will guide you into all truth. He will not speak on His own; He will speak only what He hears, and He will tell you what is yet to come. He will glorify Me because it is from Me that He will receive what He will make known to you* (John 14:15-17, 26, 16:12-14).

Ask the Holy Spirit to lead you to the truth concerning something you want to know. I did and found these verses to be true not only in spiritual matters, but also in learning sound business and professional practices that work without violating God's precepts and statutes. The Apostle Paul confirms that access to knowledge and wisdom is a direct outcome of inviting Christ into your life as Savior and Lord: *My goal is that they may be encouraged in heart and united in love, so that they may have the full riches of complete understanding, in order that they may know the mystery of God, namely, Christ, in whom are hidden all the treasures of wisdom and knowledge* (Colossians 2:2-3).

TRUTH IN THE MARKETPLACE

So how does one apply this in the marketplace? Another of Satan's core strategies is to destroy your finances – at the individual or business level - so you don't have the resources to thrive and build the Kingdom of God on earth. So let's define reality concerning sound finance. There are only two principles of finance that work and they are both Biblical:

1. **Spend less than you make,** *Why should fools have money in hand to buy wisdom, when they are not able to understand it* (Proverbs 17:16)? *Whoever loves money never has enough* (Ecclesiastes 5:10). *Ants are creatures of little strength, yet they store up their food in the summer* (Proverbs 30:25).
2. **Make more than you spend.** *The wise man saves for the future, but the foolish man spends whatever he gets* (Proverbs 21:20 TLB). *All these blessings will come upon you and accompany you if you obey the Lord your God... You will lend*

to many nations but will borrow from none (Deuteronomy 28: 2&12).

Does this seem too simple? It's the way to build wealth God's way. Proverbs 9:9 says, *Instruct the wise and they will be wiser still; teach the righteous and they will add to their learning.* I have worked with hundreds of companies and I can say with certainty that the ones that are in the top 25% of their industry are the ones that grasp that there are only two principles of finance that work and they implement them. They also build the capital and surplus earnings to 1) fund growth and development, 2) be market leaders, 3) have discretionary cash flow, 4) do humanitarian acts of mercy and grace and 5) help build the Kingdom of God. The same principles apply to individuals in managing their personal income from their career.

In Kingdom economics there are three additional critical principles that invoke God's supernatural power in your finances:

1. **Obedience.** The whole book of Deuteronomy deals with the relationship of obedience to The Promise. God's love is unconditional, but all His blessings are not, *All these blessings will come upon you and accompany you* ***if*** *you obey the LORD your God* (Deuteronomy 28:20).
2. **Tithing.** *Bring the whole tithe into the storehouse, that there may be food in My house. Test Me in this," says the Lord Almighty, "and see if I will not throw open the floodgates of heaven and pour out so much blessing that there will not be room enough to store it. I will prevent pests from devouring your crops, and the vines in your fields will not drop their fruit before it is ripe," says the Lord Almighty. "Then all the nations will call you blessed, for yours will be a delightful land" says the Lord Almighty* (Malachi 3:10-12).

3. **Belief in God's Promises.** *And without faith it is impossible to please God, because anyone who comes to Him must believe that He exists and that He rewards those who earnestly seek Him* (Hebrews 11:6).

HOW TO PUT ON YOUR BELT OF TRUTH

Following is an action plan on how to put on the Belt of Truth:

1. Read the Bible on a regular basis (start with the New Testament).
2. Load Bible software on your computer and research your questions about life and business, to help you define reality and make sound decisions.
3. Ask the Holy Spirit to lead you to the truth. His leading may include Bible passages to read, a church to attend, people to talk to, books to read, etc. Make the Bible your first priority – it is the foundation for learning Truth.
4. Memorize as much of the Bible as you are capable of, even if it is only a verse or two at a time.
5. Intentionally set your mind on what the Spirit desires by obeying the truth and basing your decisions on reality.
6. Seek His counsel continuously.
7. Apply His truth daily in thoughts, decisions and actions.
8. Do not allow Satan to derail you from this process!

FOR THE WORD OF GOD

IS LIVING AND ACTIVE.

SHARPER THAN ANY DOUBLE-EDGED SWORD,

IT PENETRATES EVEN TO

DIVIDING SOUL AND SPIRIT,

JOINTS AND MARROW;

IT JUDGES THE THOUGHTS

AND ATTITUDES

OF THE HEART.

Hebrews 4:12

But the Counselor, the Holy Spirit, who the Father will send in My name, will teach you all things and will remind you of everything I have said to you.

John 14:26

QUESTIONS FOR CONSIDERATION:

- What is the Belt of Truth? How can it help you in business?
- What are the four types of truth dealing with Spiritual Warfare and how are they important to you and your career or business?
- How is Satan lying to you? What impact is that having on your life, career or business?
- How do you "put on" the Belt of Truth?
- What Scriptures can you use to overcome Satan when he attacks you?

Above all else, guard your heart, for
everything you do flows from it.
Proverbs 4:23
THE
BREASTPLATE
OF
RIGHTEOUSNESS

CHAPTER 5

THE BREASTPLATE OF RIGHTEOUSNESS

The Armor of God enables you to stand against the devil's schemes because the weapons we wield have supernatural power to demolish strongholds and keep your heart protected!

PUTTING ON THE BREASTPLATE OF RIGHTEOUSNESS

Satan's name, which means adversary or *diabolos,* translated devil, which means accuser, is a clue to one of his Key Schemes. He uses accusations, creating legitimate and/or false guilt to keep us down. Therefore, Satan loves to make us feel inadequate in our Christian walk, discouraging us from growing spiritually, thus diminishing or even eliminating our Kingdom effectiveness. Let's review some examples from Chapter 3:

- Satan does his best to find something he can make us feel guilty about because he knows that a Christian who feels guilty is discouraged and ineffective.
- Satan uses accusations to destroy trust and unity in

relationships - especially in churches, families and the Body of Christ.

- Satan will jump at any opportunity to convince us to focus on the guilt our failures produce instead of Christ's redeeming work of grace at the cross.

How do we defend ourselves against these schemes? With the Breastplate of Righteousness! First, let's look at the function of a breastplate:

"The breastplate was a central part of the Roman soldier's armor—it provided protection for the torso, which contains vital organs like the heart, lungs and so on. Without a breastplate, a soldier would be asking for death, as any attack could instantly become fatal. With a sturdy breastplate, the very same attacks become ineffective and useless, as blows glance off the armor. Without righteousness, we leave ourselves open to almost certain death. With righteousness—just as with a breastplate—the otherwise fatal attacks of our enemy are thwarted."[1]

There are two forms of righteousness the Bible refers to:

» **Imputed righteousness** is a free gift from Christ to those who receive Him into their life as Savior and Lord, asking forgiveness for their sins and accepting God's free gift of Christ's righteousness. This righteousness is accredited to them through His death on the cross where He paid the penalty for their sins. As a result of this gift, you are righteous in God's eyes. *Now when a man works, his wages are not credited to him as a gift, but as an obligation. However, to the man who does not work but trusts God who justifies the wicked, his faith is credited as righteousness* (Romans 4:4-5). This is a singular event in your life and it NEVER changes. Once you become a child of God, the penalty for your sins (past, present

1 www.freebiblestudyguides.org

and future) is paid for and you are made righteous in God's eyes.

» **Imparted righteousness** is a process (referred to as sanctification) of learning how to live in your earthly "body of sin." This is accomplished through the power of the Holy Spirit living in you. As you *walk in the Spirit,* Christ's righteousness is imparted to you. In other words, you are taught how to live righteously every day of your life through the power of Christ inside you! This is a continuous process that enables you to live more and more like Christ daily.

Knowing how to deal with Satan's schemes involves the following:

» **Renewing** your mind by using the Action Plan in Chapter 4. This results in removing the lies that Satan and the world have programmed into you during your lifetime and replacing them with truth about reality as found in the Bible (the way things actually are versus the way you think they are or the way Satan wants you to believe they are). Some verses to help you do that are:

  * *Do not conform to the pattern of this world, but be transformed by the renewing of your mind* (Romans 12:2).

  * *All Scripture is God-breathed and is useful for teaching, rebuking, correcting and training in righteousness* (2 Timothy 3:16).

  * *My goal is that they may be encouraged in heart and united in love, so that they may have the full riches of complete understanding, in order that they may know the mystery of God, namely, Christ, in Whom are hidden all the treasures of wisdom and knowledge* (Colossians 2:2-3).

» **Believing** that you can *live as Jesus did* (1 John 2:6) on this earth by trusting Christ to render your flesh powerless and by setting your mind (making a permanent decision) to walk everyday under the influence, power and leading of the Spirit of God living in you.

» **Committing** to the spiritual growth process that follows.

You now know that godliness is attainable! How do you know? The Bible tells you so. *For this very reason, make every effort to add to your faith goodness; and to goodness, knowledge; and to knowledge, self-control; and to self-control, perseverance; and to perseverance, godliness* (2 Peter 1:5-6).

As you go through the sanctification process, remember that only God can make you godly or holy. You cannot get up in the morning and decide to be more godly. Godliness is a work of God. *Consider the lilies of the field, how they grow: they neither toil nor spin* (Matthew 6:28b NKJV).

Jesus is telling us that only God makes things grow and the Apostle Paul confirms this: *I planted the seed, Apollos watered it,* ***but God made it grow.*** *So neither he who plants nor he who waters is anything,* ***but only God, who makes things grow*** (1 Corinthians 3:6-8).

Our job is to cooperate with Him by believing daily that He is with us and assisting us, *Jesus answered, 'The work of God is this: to believe in the one He has sent'* (John 6:29). God designed it this way so you will seek Him, stay humble and not become prideful. [2] We can achieve holiness because we have a "new nature," therefore we have the ability to make the right choices. *But now that you have been set free from sin and have become slaves of God, the benefit you reap leads to holiness, and the result is eternal life* Romans 6:22).

The Apostle John also instructs us in this regard as he gives us guidelines as to who the children of God really are. *We know that we*

2 See 2 Corinthians 12:7-9 to see how Paul handled this.

have come to know Him if we keep His commands. Whoever says, "I know Him," but does not do what He commands is a liar, and the truth is not in that person. But if anyone obeys His word, love for God is truly made complete in them. This is how we know we are in Him: Whoever claims to live in Him must live as Jesus did (1 John 2:3-6).

SATAN'S SCHEMES TO DERAIL YOUR SANCTIFICATION PROCESS

Satan will attack you with accusations of how bad or weak a person you are because you continue to sin after becoming a born again Christian. He will convince you that there is no hope of you ever attaining godliness and tell you to give up and stop pretending to be a Christian. You will likely feel grieved in your soul, because this is contrary to how God sees you. Despite your failures, God's Spirit still lives within you. With love, the Spirit gently convicts you of your sin and you will want to stop sinning because you want to please and serve God.

But as soon as you are convicted, Satan turns up the heat. He continues to accuse you of being a bad person encouraging you to question whether you are really a Christian. This is easy for Satan to do because he knows that you have to go through a sanctification process and that you will continue to sin, even though you are sinning less as you learn to "walk in the spirit" and "put on your new nature."

To make himself more believable, Satan has already convinced millions of Christians that becoming godly is impossible, so they discourage you from trying. This only supports Satan's lie. This is very bad for the Body of Christ, because people will not attempt to achieve something they believe to be impossible. And that is why the forces of darkness are currently winning the war in the Body of Christ. If God says it's possible, then it is possible! So choose to believe Him and stand on His truth when Satan and his followers try to discourage you and persuade you otherwise.

My wife and I have a few friends who have divorced their spouses and married other people. Over the years we tried to counsel them not to do it. But they had their minds set on what their flesh desired, instead of God's word, so they justified their sin with a whole list of rationalizations provided by the enemy and proceeded with their divorces. Several years afterward, most of them confided in me that they had made a big mistake and wished they hadn't done it. They explained they still loved their first spouse. They also confessed that their relationships with their children and old friends were not the same and they should have listened to counsel.

I once attended a team building workshop, where they taught us that building a team is a growth process. One of the phases in this process is called the "storming phase." During this phase there is a lot of conflict and stress as the members learn to communicate better, work together effectively and trust each other at a deeper level. This is a perfectly normal phase in the development of a team, but it is needful and should be expected. It's important for team members to not get discouraged and give up on each other. They need to persevere and the members will come together as a team.

Likewise, husbands and wives must learn to function as a team. The Bible says, *the two will become one* (Matthew 19:5)! So be patient with your spouse (well, be patient with everyone, but especially your spouse) and set your minds together to work through the "storming phase." Remember that your struggle is not against flesh and blood.

I can personally testify to the importance of learning this truth. In early 1970, the enemy convinced me that I didn't love my wife and that our marriage was hopeless. I had no peace. Life was not going well with Ree Ann and me at all. So I left her and the boys to find "happiness." The third night I was gone, the Lord spoke to me: "It is time for you to decide if you are going to serve Me or not." I recognized His voice and immediately called Ree Ann and asked her if I could come back. She graciously and immediately said yes.

Although I had not gone to church for several years, as soon as I got home I picked up the Bible my father had given me as a child and began searching for verses concerning "peace." One verse jumped off the page at me: *If you raise up your family in the way of the Lord, you shall have peace.* If one thing was lacking in my family at that point, it was peace. I knew I had to make some changes. I decided to start going to church again and have done so ever since. Amazingly, I have never been able to find that verse again and honestly don't know if it was really there or if the Holy Spirit just had me see a verse that way. This may sound strange to you, but it is true.

Looking back to that time, I am amazed at just how good Satan is at his lies and deception. Ree Ann was, is and always will be "the love of my life." And I am very grateful that God got us safely through that period of darkness. Our love for one another was restored and we learned to work together as a team. Since then, we have prospered in every way - spiritually, emotionally, financially and relationally – as we worked side by side in the business domain.

In 2009, I was meeting with a senior level manager who had been a Christian all his life. He held positions in senior level management and leadership - in both business and religious non-profit organizations. He taught adult Sunday School for several years. I would rank him in the top 1% of gifted leaders/managers that I have known. About twenty years prior to our meeting, he was involved in an affair that led to him losing a job in one of the fastest growing successful companies in America. He repented to his wife and God and continued with a series of successful jobs, but his success was never quite the same.

Over the years he began to question if the Apostle Paul's teaching on righteousness was attainable. And his relationship with his wife drifted apart. When I met with him in 2009 we were discussing the topic of the holiness of the believer, Paul's words in Ephesians 5:3-6 being a key part of that discussion: *But among you there must not be even a hint of sexual immorality, or of any kind of impurity, or of greed, because these are improper for God's holy people. Nor should there be obscenity, foolish talk or coarse joking, which are out of place, but rather thanksgiving. For of this you can be sure: No immoral, impure or greedy person — such a person is an idolater — has any inheritance in the Kingdom of Christ and of God. Let no one deceive you with empty words, for because of such things God's wrath comes on those who are disobedient.*

"That is not possible!" he declared to me. I asked him if he thought God would ask us to do something that was not possible. He said, "Well, just look around you in Christianity! There is evidence everywhere that it is not possible." I could see that Satan had won the war with him. We talked some more and I tried to reason with him but he was not listening. In 2012, he divorced his wife and the following year, married another woman. Since 2009, he has worked at nothing but odd jobs – every one of them far beneath his former successes.

You see, God's love is unconditional but His blessings under the Covenant Promise are not. Like any corporate culture, the Kingdom Culture rewards people who comply with its ways, *All these blessings will come on you and accompany you if you obey the Lord your God - However, if you do not obey the Lord your God...all these curses will come on you and overtake you* (Deuteronomy 28:2 and 15).

After 29 years of business consulting, I can most assuredly tell you that people will not do something they believe to be impossible. Satan is counting on that. It's his core strategy when it comes to righteousness and holiness - to get you to believe that achieving them is impossible, which leads to a decline in your obedience and God's protection and blessing in your life.

STANDING FIRM AFTER PUTTING ON YOUR BREASTPLATE OF RIGHTEOUSNESS

If you persevere, you will sin less and less, while intentional sin becomes very infrequent. When Satan comes at you with accusations, quote the following Scriptures to him, saying, *"Satan, it is written!"* Then stand firm on its truth:

» **Christ's righteousness has been credited to me.** *Those who receive God's abundant provision of grace and of the gift of righteousness reign in life through the one man, Jesus Christ* (Romans 5:17).

» **Christ's righteousness is being imparted to me as I learn to walk as He walked. God is not finished with me yet.** *I have been crucified with Christ and I no longer live, but Christ lives in me. The life I live in the body, I live by faith in the Son of God, Who loved me and gave Himself for me. I do not set aside the grace of God, for if righteousness could be gained through the law* (works), *Christ died for nothing* (Galatians 2:20-21)!

» **It is possible to live a righteous life.** *His divine power has given us everything we need for life and godliness through our knowledge of Him who called us by His own glory and goodness* (2 Peter 1:3).

To defeat the forces of darkness, believe that God's wisdom will work in your life. Keep your relationship with Christ healthy by applying these truths daily:

» To stand firm when Satan attacks you, the first thing you need to do is to make sure you know you are not guilty.

When you do sin, confess your sin to God immediately (1 John 1:9). Once you have done that, He is faithful and just to forgive your sin. Now you can know you are in right standing with Christ.

» Keep your mind set on what the Spirit desires so you disobey God less frequently. When you do disobey, follow the process above and reset your mind on what the Spirit desires. Then send Satan packing!

» When the devil tempted Christ in Luke 4:1-13, Christ had His mind set on what His Father desired, so He said no to Satan after each of his efforts to appeal to Christ's human nature.

» To send Satan packing, Christ ALWAYS used Scripture, and ONLY Scripture, to say no and take His stand against the devil. You can – and MUST - do the same!

Following are a few keys to standing firm that you also can use on a daily basis:

1. **Withhold your anger at yourself or others.** *Our struggle is not against flesh and blood* (Ephesians 6:12). *"In your anger do not sin": Do not let the sun go down while you are still angry, and do not give the devil a foothold* (Ephesians 4:26-27).
2. **Disregard any spirit or person who tells you godliness is not attainable.** *But just as He who called you is holy, so be holy in all you do* (1 Peter 1:15).
3. **Confess your sin to God.** *If we confess our sins, He is faithful and just and will forgive us our sins and purify us from all unrighteousness* (1 John 1:9).
4. **Set your mind** on what the Spirit desires (Romans 8:5) and *walk in the Spirit in your new nature.*
5. **Rejoice in the Lord always.** *I will say it again: Rejoice! Let your gentleness be evident to all. The Lord is near. Do not be anxious about anything, but in every situation, by prayer and petition, with thanksgiving, present your*

> *requests to God. And the peace of God, which transcends all understanding, will guard your hearts and your minds in Christ Jesus. Finally, brothers and sisters, whatever is true, whatever is noble, whatever is right, whatever is pure, whatever is lovely, whatever is admirable — if anything is excellent or praiseworthy — think about such things* (Philippians 4:4-8).

Like Christ, stand your ground! He knew Satan feared God the Father and that Satan would give up and go away if He stood on and had faith in God's Word. *When the devil had finished all this tempting, he left Him until an opportune time* (Luke 4:13).

Recall that sanctification is a process, not an event, so keep at it until you develop judgment on how to take your stand against the devil's schemes and successfully complete the process in 2 Peter 1:5-9!

When Satan comes at you with accusations for sins you have already asked God to forgive, making you feel guilty because of your day-to-day mistakes, quote Scripture to him and say, **"Go away Satan, Christ died on the Cross for that mistake and by the way, God gives me His Grace to make mistakes – He isn't finished with me yet!"**

AND THE GOD OF ALL GRACE,

**WHO CALLED YOU TO HIS ETERNAL GLORY IN CHRIST,
AFTER YOU HAVE SUFFERED A LITTLE WHILE,
WILL HIMSELF RESTORE YOU
AND MAKE YOU STRONG, FIRM AND STEADFAST.
TO HIM BE THE POWER FOR EVER AND EVER.
AMEN.**

The Apostle Peter

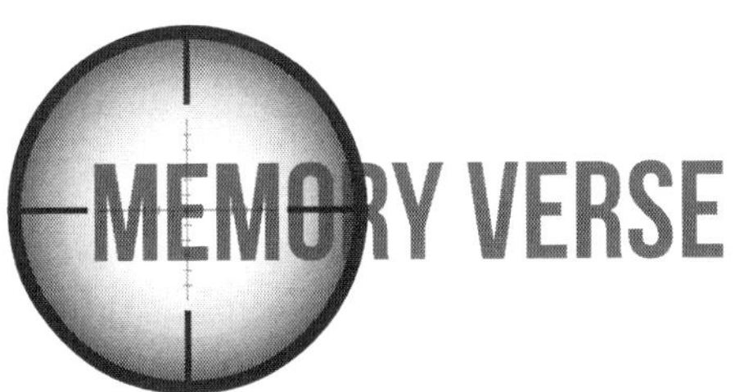

I have been crucified with Christ and I no longer live, but Christ lives in me. The life I now live in the body, I live by faith in the Son of God, Who loved me and gave Himself for me. I do not set aside the grace of God, for if righteousness could be gained through the law, Christ died for nothing!

Galatians 2:20-21

QUESTIONS FOR CONSIDERATION:

- What is the Breastplate of Righteousness?
- How was Christ's righteousness imputed to you?
- How is Christ's righteousness imparted to you?
- What scheme(s) is Satan using to destroy your sanctification process? What difference does it make to the success of your career or business?
- How can you take your stand against these schemes?

The God of peace will soon crush Satan underneath your feet.
Romans 16:20
THE
GOSPEL
OF
PEACE

CHAPTER 6

THE GOSPEL OF PEACE

The Great Commission is an imperative calling Christians to build the Kingdom of God on earth by making disciples. *Then Jesus came to them and said, "All authority in heaven and on earth has been given to Me. Therefore go and make disciples of all nations, baptizing them in the name of the Father and of the Son and of the Holy Spirit, and teaching them to obey everything I have commanded you. And surely I am with you always, to the very end of the age"* (Matthew 28:18-20).

Satan is very intentional about dissuading you from Christ's Mission because it brings life, peace and power to others. If you are in any way involved personally or professionally in sharing the Gospel and making disciples, you had better know the enemy and how to defend yourself against him or he will make every effort to make your life miserable. The Gospel of Peace will give you and your disciples a sure footing to stand on when facing the enemy's attacks.

FITTING YOUR FEET WITH THE GOSPEL OF PEACE

The Apostle Paul instructs us to fit our feet with the Gospel of Peace so Satan can't derail us from being effective in building the Kingdom of God on earth. Protecting your feet is crucial to your health, protection and comfort in battle. If you can't move around confidently and comfortably, you leave yourself vulnerable to an agile enemy. "A shoeless soldier could run into real trouble in the heat of battle. Unless he is fighting on Astroturf, he is going to encounter some debris. To a bare foot that can cause serious pain—and one of the last things you want to deal with in the middle of a fight is worrying about where you can step. Just as shoes allow us to walk on otherwise painful terrain without fear, so too the preparation of the Gospel of Peace allows us to traverse the otherwise painful trials and tribulations of life without fear, knowing that what awaits is greater than anything we could possibly suffer in this world." [1]*I consider that our present sufferings are not worth comparing with the glory that will be revealed in us* (Romans 8:18).

The more you obey The Great Commission and The Great Commandment, *Love each other as I have loved you* (John 15:12), the more Satan will try to create a lack of peace in your mind, your emotions and your relationships. Pastor Parker says that Satan's "chief objective is to knock us down, while our primary goal is to remain standing."

As we switch from defense to offense by taking the Gospel into the marketplace, we must have a good foundation to stand on in order to work in the power and authority of Christ while enduring the enemy's onslaught. Knowing that God is with us and has provided a way for us to be at peace with Him – through Jesus – we are able

1 www.freebiblestudyguides.org

to experience that peace and face whatever the enemy may hurl our way. *Therefore, since we have been justified through faith, we have peace with God through our Lord Jesus Christ* (Romans 5:1).

BATTLES AND STRUGGLES IN THIS LIFE

When you share the Gospel of Peace with others and they accept Christ into their life as Savior and Lord, you are putting on Gospel shoes, which make you special in the Kingdom of God. *How beautiful...are the feet of those who bring good news, who proclaim peace* (Isaiah 52:7)! You bring true peace into the life of another person by inviting them into God's family and introducing them to Kingdom citizenship.

As you recall, Christians are engaged in three struggles in this life against: The Sinful Nature (sin living in you); The devil (Satan); and The World.

The struggles with Satan and the Sinful Nature have been discussed already, so let's examine our struggle with the world.

THE WORLD AND TRIBULATIONS

Nelson's Illustrated Bible Dictionary has this to say about the trials we face in the world: "The Bible warns against philosophies whose highest realities and concerns are atoms, energy, cosmic laws, or humanity - those founded on *the elemental spiritual forces of this world, rather than on Christ* (Colossians 2:8). Christians ought to beware that their minds are not taken captive by such philosophies as secular humanism, communist materialism and capitalist materialism. These philosophies are best fought with spiritual weapons. *For though we live in the world, we do not wage war as the world does. The weapons we fight with are not the weapons of the world* (2 Corinthians 10:3-4).

"Christian wisdom appears to be foolishness to the people of the world (1 Corinthians 1:18). But God is wiser than the philosophy of this age, which comes to nothing (1 Corinthians 1:25; 2:6).

"Christians *speak the wisdom of God* (1 Corinthians 2:7 NKJV), which is revealed through His Spirit (1 Corinthians 2:10) and received by His Spirit (1 Corinthians 2:12-14). Christians have the highest and most complete wisdom in Christ (Ephesians 1:17).

"Satan's influence in worldly affairs is also clearly revealed (John 12:31). His various titles reflect his control of the world system: *the prince of this world* (John 12:31), *the god of this age* (2 Corinthians 4:4) and *the ruler of the kingdom of the air* (Ephesians 2:2). The Bible declares, *The whole world is under the control of the evil one* (1 John 5:19)."

Since the world operates under belief systems that are a mixture of God's truth, Satan's lies and man's philosophies, the children of God – those who stand on God's truth alone - do not fit into this world any better than Christ did. So you can expect to encounter tribulation while living in Satan's domain. *If the world hates you, keep in mind that it hated Me first. If you belonged to the world, it would love you as its own. As it is, you do not belong to the world, but I have chosen you out of the world. That is why the world hates you. Remember what I told you: 'A servant is not greater than his master.' If they persecuted Me, they will persecute you also. If they obeyed My teaching, they will obey yours also. They will treat you this way because of My name, for they do not know the One Who sent Me* (John 15:18-21).

You can obtain peace in the midst of this tribulation by "keeping your eyes on Jesus" (something my earthly father taught me). Christ said *I have told you these things, so that in Me you may have peace. In this world you will have trouble. But take heart! I have overcome the world. God's prophet Isaiah assures us, You will keep him in perfect peace whose mind is stayed on You* (Isaiah 26:3 NKJV).

SATAN'S POWER VS. GOD'S POWER

It is imperative that we know our enemy and his schemes! As an archangel, Satan had significant power. Despite his falling from grace, he is still powerful enough that Michael the archangel viewed him as a foe too powerful to oppose directly (Jude 9). Satan exercises that power through demons, his agents of evil (Matthew 12:24, 25:41). He is also highly intelligent, as evidenced by his deception of Adam and Eve so he could gain authority over this world (Genesis 3:1-7). Yet, Satan does not possess unlimited power. He is still subject to God's power and restrictions on his activities (Job 1:7-12).

Even with Satan's power and intelligence, you can overcome him and have peace in your heart and mind. *After all, the One Who is in you is greater than the one who is in the world* (1 John 4:4). *'Does Job fear God for nothing?' Satan replied. 'Have You not put a hedge around him and his household and everything he has? You have blessed the work of his hands, so that his flocks and herds are spread throughout the land'* (Job 1:9-10). No matter what you face, God is always enough!

Ironically, putting the Gospel of Peace on our feet is an offensive tactic as well as a defensive one. Romans 16:20 says, *The God of Peace will soon crush Satan under your feet.* Peace not only becomes our protection, but a weapon against the enemy!

SUFFERING AND TRIALS - A TALE OF TWO PARTNERSHIPS

Partnerships, as beneficial as they are, can bring a lot of stress, temptations and testing into your life. Years ago I was working with a partnership of two Christian men who had built a very successful business over about fifteen years. The economy went into a downturn and business fell off significantly, putting a lot of financial pressure on the two owners. They became very angry and self-seeking, looking for the worst in each other. They contacted me for help. One of my business associates (who specialized in management and conflict resolution) and I advised them to see past the current circumstances, put their trust in God and His teaching, and focus on working together to get through the downturn. We even suggested they see an industrial psychologist who specialized in conflict resolution in business. Filled with anger, one of the partners refused to cooperate with any suggestions or recommendations. Nothing we tried would penetrate his anger. It was "his way or the highway." He bought the other partner out (on his terms) and the company failed. He didn't do it God's way and Satan won that battle.

A few years later I was working with another partnership comprised of two Christian men who had also built a successful business over about twenty years. One of the partners became burned out and was not carrying his weight in the business. As a result, the other one became frustrated and angry. He saw an opportunity to grow the business even more. Their two objectives became divided. However, they were both committed to following Christ and they began to pray about the situation and seek business and spiritual counsel from myself and others. At my recommendation, they hired the industrial psychologist specializing in conflict resolution. The owner who was burned out hired a personal psychologist to help him through his burnout.

Working together over several months, the burned out partner recovered, the other partner was patient, and together they made some compromises. We formulated a new strategic business plan that they both committed to. By putting their trust in God, advisors and each other, they restored their relationship and built their company into a very profitable industry leader. They did it God's way and Satan lost.

Sin and suffering came into the world when Adam fell in the Garden and gave his authority over to the devil (Genesis 3:16-19). Some suffering, however, is beneficial in that it serves to shape and refine us (1 Peter 1:6-7). The Bible says Jesus Himself benefited from His sufferings, learning obedience (Hebrews 5:8).

Suffering puts us in a position to be a comfort to others who are suffering (2 Corinthians 1:3-6). Suffering also helps us to identify with Christ and brings us into a closer bond with Him (Philippians 3:10).

No one likes suffering and trials. But if you trust God's ways, you will like the outcome!

» *Submit to God and be at peace with Him; in this way prosperity will come to you (Job 22:21).*

» *A heart at peace gives life to the body, but envy rots the bones (Proverbs 14:30).*

» *He said to her, "Daughter, your faith has healed you. Go in peace and be freed from your suffering" (Mark 5:34).*

THE GOSPEL OF PEACE LIGHTENS OUR SUFFERING!

People on Planet Earth have sufficient suffering, trials and tribulations to make their lives turbulent, stressful and painful. So what is the solution? The Gospel of Peace!

God's children are called to broadcast the good news of God's Kingdom. Putting on our gospel shoes of peace, we are prepared to walk as Jesus walked (1 John 2:6) and spread the Gospel of Peace to others. *How then shall they call on Him in Whom they have not believed? And how shall they believe in Him of Whom they have not heard? And how shall they hear without a preacher? And how shall they preach unless they are sent? As it is written: 'How beautiful are the feet of those who preach the gospel of peace, who bring glad tidings of good things'* (Romans 10:14-15 NKJV)!

When Satan attacks you, when your job is filled with stress, when relationships are stressed, when the world hates you, and when you feel you are losing the battle with life, Satan or your sinful nature, stand on and believe in the Word of God (the Gospel of Peace) and you will have peace in the midst of suffering, trials and tribulation as you live through your sanctification process.

When you choose to believe the Gospel of Peace, you are putting on your Gospel Shoes and you will have peace because:

* You no longer doubt God's love (Romans 8:38-39).
* You obey God (John 15:9-17).
* You have complete understanding (Colossians 2:2-3).
* You no longer fear death (Romans 8:38-39).
* You have victory over Satan (Revelation 12:10-11).
* You understand how to have victory over your sin nature (Romans 8:1-17).
* You no longer fear God's judgment or hell (1 John 5:13).
* You no longer have to fear man or the forces of darkness (Romans 8:28-31 and Psalm 56:11).
* You no longer fear that your life counts for nothing (1 Corinthians 15:58).
* You participate in God's divine nature (2 Peter 1:3-4).
* You will have sincere love for others (1 Peter 1:22).
* You will experience the abundant life (John 10:10).
* You know deep in your heart who you are - a child of God, the Father Almighty (1 John 3:1)!

STANDING FIRM AFTER PUTTING ON YOUR GOSPEL SHOES

When Satan fills your heart with fear and doubt, hold firm to the Gospel of Peace. *Now, brothers and sisters, I want to remind you of the gospel I preached to you, which you received and on which you have taken your stand. By this gospel you are saved, if you hold firmly to the word I preached to you. Otherwise, you have believed in vain* (1 Corinthians 15:1-2). The following will help you stand firm:

Remember whose power to draw on. *Do not be afraid or discouraged because of this vast army. For the battle is not yours, but God's* (2 Chronicles 20:15b).

Trust God's sanctification process. *For we know that our old self was crucified with Him so that the body ruled by sin might be done away with, that we should no longer be slaves to sin — because anyone who has died has been set free from sin. Now if we died with Christ, we believe that we will also live with Him* (Romans 6:6-8).

Rely on the power of Christ living in you, *I have been crucified with Christ and I no longer live, but Christ lives in me. The life I now live in the body (of sin), I live by faith in the Son of God, who loved me and gave Himself for me. I do not set aside the grace of God, for if righteousness could be gained through the law, Christ died for nothing* (Galatians 2:20-21)!

You are a child of the Almighty God. He is with you!

IF GOD IS FOR US,

WHO CAN BE AGAINST US?
NO, IN ALL THESE THINGS
WE ARE MORE THAN CONQUERORS
THROUGH HIM WHO LOVED US.
FOR I AM CONVINCED
THAT NEITHER DEATH NOR LIFE,
NEITHER ANGELS NOR DEMONS,
NEITHER THE PRESENT NOR THE FUTURE,
NOR ANY POWERS,
NEITHER HEIGHT NOR DEPTH,
NOR ANYTHING ELSE IN ALL CREATION,
WILL BE ABLE TO SEPARATE US
FROM THE LOVE OF GOD
THAT IS IN CHRIST JESUS OUR LORD.

The Apostle Paul

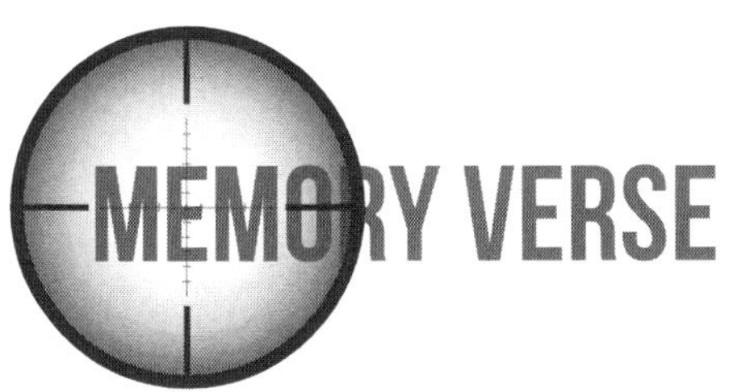

Now, brothers and sisters,
I want to remind you of the gospel I preached to you,
which you received and on which you have taken
your stand. By this gospel you are saved, if you hold
firmly to the word I preached to you.
Otherwise, you have believed in vain.

1 Corinthians 15:1-2

QUESTIONS FOR CONSIDERATION:

- What is the Gospel of Peace?
- What are your three primary struggles?
- How do you put on your Gospel Shoes in Business?
- What are the benefits of putting on your Gospel Shoes?
- What is your action plan for walking in peace?

Above all, taking the shield of faith with which you will be able to quench all the fiery darts of the wicked one.

Ephesians 6:16

THE SHIELD OF FAITH

CHAPTER 7

THE SHIELD OF FAITH

In men's Bible study years ago, I heard Dr. Bob Beltz discuss that, "Most Christians believe their problems are too big and God is too small." Not trusting God by following His teachings can lead to this perspective, resulting in an even greater lack of faith.

That's one reason I am writing this book, to encourage Christians to build up their awareness of the cosmic war they are engaged in and increase their skills in accessing the enormous power God has to protect them in their daily lives.

Satan wants you to lose faith in God and break fellowship with Him. The Bible says you can overcome him and the forces of darkness by putting on the full Armor of God daily. Over time, as you demonstrate your faith in God by following His commands and teaching, you will experience and recognize the enormous power God has to protect and bless you.

All of the Armor's defenses and offenses are founded on faith in

God and His honor to keep His Promise.

PUTTING ON THE SHIELD OF FAITH

God is not moved by our needs, He is moved by our faith. In 1 Samuel 17:45, faced with overwhelming insurmountable odds in the form of Goliath, David's first words toward his enemy are: *You come against me with sword and spear and javelin, but I come against you in the name of the Lord Almighty, the God of the armies of Israel, whom you have defied. This day the Lord will deliver you into my hands, and I'll strike you down and cut off your head* (1 Samuel 17:45-46). As you know, David defeated the Philistine with a single stone. Who was David at the time? He was a shepherd working in the business domain, tending his father's sheep.

The Apostle Paul instructs us that God's eternal purpose was accomplished in Christ Jesus our Lord and therefore, *In Him and through faith in Him we may approach God with freedom and confidence* (Ephesians 3:12). What would it look like, then, to have a shield of faith?

"The Roman shield - the *scutum* - was not the standard "medieval-esque" shield most picture in their minds upon hearing the word. It was instead a very large, slightly curved rectangular shield featuring at its center a large metal knob (called a boss).

"The *scutum* was an impressive line of defense. Because of its sheer size (some were three and a half feet tall and almost three feet wide); soldiers were afforded a great deal of protection from enemies. Because of its slight curve, it was able to deflect attacks without transferring the full force of the assault to the man holding the shield. Because of its boss, it was able to deflect even the more vicious blows and function in a limited offensive capacity as a means of knocking an opponent backwards." [1]

Faith is taking God at His word and acting on it! Faith is real and based on indisputable truth. The Bible says that *faith is the substance of things hoped for, the evidence of things not seen* (Hebrews 11:1 NKJV). We think of faith as an abstract concept, but the writer of Hebrews says that it is a concrete substance, and that the evidence is solid proof. Faith, then, is not based on emotion or feelings, but on concrete proof – on reality. *For we were saved in this hope, but hope that is seen is not hope; for why does one still hope for what he sees? But if we hope for what we do not see, we eagerly wait for it with perseverance* (Romans 8:24-25 NKJV).

This doesn't mean, of course, that faith comes easily or naturally. We have spent our whole life in this world and therefore our mind and soul are very influenced by the tangible environment we live in, our experiences and the false evidence Satan orchestrates. Paul's point is that you do not hope for what you already can see. Faith requires a large degree of trust. Trust in what? That part of the evidence around you that proves that there is a God and He is very powerful and trustworthy. Who is more trustworthy than God, the Father?

By searching the Scriptures, observing creation, considering the testimonies of God's faithfulness to us and others in the faith, we deduce that God has proven Himself constant, unchanging, and trustworthy over the millennia. Then we are encouraged to exercise our faith that He will build our faith and fulfill His promises to us. Some of our experiences would indicate otherwise. However, we can choose to stand on our faith in God's character until He helps us overcome our unbelief through His faithfulness!

To put this in terms we understand in the business domain,

1 www.freebiblestudyguides.org

in world governments, money is the currency by which power and authority is bought, rewards are paid and favor is received. But in the Kingdom of God, faith is the currency by which God's favor is received and His power, authority and blessings are increased in your life.

FIVE CHARACTERISTICS OF THE SHIELD OF FAITH

1. **A shield is the first line of defense.** Pastor Shafer Parker says that the shield "was used by the Romans to ward off the opening barrage from the enemy. Using bows or catapults, the enemy would shoot flaming arrows, throw fireballs, fling rough metal darts covered in flaming pitch, all for the purpose of overwhelming the other side, to create chaos and confusion." The devil tries to do the same thing to us individually, in congregations and in the Church as a whole. Just look at the barrage of lies and moral attacks on the Body of Christ today. Satan will do anything to derail a person's faith and trust in God to stop the advance of God's Kingdom on earth. Even as a young boy, David knew to pull out his shield of faith first before brandishing any weaponry.
2. **A shield guards.** Christ, as the great High Priest, who understands our weaknesses and vulnerabilities, stands guard over us. *The One Who was born of God keeps them safe, and the evil one cannot harm them* (1 John 5:18).
3. **A shield deflects.** Faith in God and His promises extinguishes Satan's flaming arrows, so he is unable to penetrate our mind and soul. *Because God wanted to make the unchanging nature of His purpose very clear to the heirs of what was promised, He confirmed it with an oath. God did this so that, by two unchangeable things in which it is impossible for God to lie, we who have fled to take hold of the hope set before us may be greatly encouraged. We have this hope as an anchor for the soul, firm and secure* (Hebrews 6:17-19a). *He will cover you with his feathers, and under His wings you will find refuge; His faithfulness*

will be your shield and rampart. You will not fear the terror of night, nor the arrow that flies by day, nor the pestilence that stalks in the darkness, nor the plague that destroys at midday (Psalm 91:4-6).

4. **A shield can incapacitate the enemy.** Jesus was able to shut the devil down using His faith in the Father and knowledge of the Word: *Jesus said to him, 'Away from me, Satan! For it is written: "Worship the Lord your God, and serve Him only."' Then the devil left Him, and angels came and attended Him* (Matthew 4:10-11).
5. **There is strength in numbers of shields.** By banding together with others in unity, faith and prayer, you create a large powerful composite shield to thwart Satan's flaming arrows. "The Roman military had an inventive and very effective tactic that made use of their large shields. When enemies would begin firing arrows and other projectiles at the army, the soldiers would close ranks into a rectangular array—called the *testudo*, or "tortoise," formation—and those on the outside would use their shields to create a wall around the perimeter. Then those in the middle would raise their shields over their heads to protect everyone from airborne missiles. The result was a formidable human tank that could be stopped only through a tremendous effort." [2]

We should also not overlook the importance of the Roman military unit moving as one. Thomas Reid said "a chain is only as strong as its weakest link." Likewise, the *testudo* formation is only effective if every soldier is working in sync with his compatriots. To exercise a different plan than the group - in this situation could be a matter of life or death! Similarly, as Christians on the battle lines, we are most effective when we "add our faith" to that of our fellow soldiers and advance the Kingdom together.

---

2 www.freebiblestudyguides.org

TEMPTATIONS

Sometimes God tests our faith by allowing the devil to tempt us. In the case of Job, Jesus Christ, Peter and many others in Scripture, God allowed bad things to happen to good men.

Pastor Parker explains this, "What does all this mean for me and you? Well, it at least means that we should not be shocked when we are attacked by the devil. It doesn't mean God has forgotten us. Nor does it mean we're doomed. In fact, these stories tell us that attacks from Satan are a part of God's plan for each of our lives. Think of it like this. None of these men would have known the victory of God had they not suffered for God. None would have known the power of God had they not come to the end of their own strength." *For the battle is not yours, but God's* (2 Chronicles 20:15).

Parker makes the observation that Satan attacked each of these three men of faith through their flesh. He is using the same avenue today. Whether it's to entice us through our desires or flog us with our fears, our flesh is quick to respond. The only sure way to recognize his temptations is to listen to the counsel of the Holy Spirit and develop a keen sense of right and wrong that can readily identify the source of his suggestions. We do this by learning, through practice, to recognize the voice of God intimately so that we can discern whether a suggestion comes from above or from below. Knowing God's voice strengthens our faith. When Satan flings his flaming arrows at us from afar, our Shield of Faith wards them off.

I saw this manifested in my own life. After several years of conscious spiritual war, exhaustion set in from not seeing the results that I had been expecting. In a moment of great frustration, I declared to the Lord, "I am sick of this continuous spiritual warfare and I don't want to do it anymore!" His response was quick, loving and to the point. "Tough!" He said, "It's just the way it is, so get over it." "Ok, I get it," I responded. From that day forward I completely turned it over to the Lord and the exhaustion and frustration have gone away. I had finally come to the end of my own strength and therefore made the real decision to put on the armor of God and move on. For people with leadership talents, this is considerably harder than we think.

FLAMING ARROWS

The flaming arrows of the evil one are no ordinary temptations. Pastor Parker says they are "things that seem to suddenly come from nowhere to pierce and penetrate and torment the soul." Satan is an intelligent being. He knows exactly what to hit us with.

Martin Luther, the great Reformer, once was battling it out with Satan. The spiritual battle was so real that Luther picked up an ink well full of black ink and threw it so it splattered against a white wall. The ink stain is no longer there (actually, no one is able to support that it actually happened). But Luther did often say that he had driven the devil away with ink.

In *The Seal and Pledge of the Holy Spirit,* Brian Allison reports "The devil sought to discourage [Luther], by making him feel guilty, through rehearsing a list of his sins. When the devil had finished, Luther purportedly said, 'Think harder: you must have forgotten some.' And the devil did think, and he listed more sins. When he was done enumerating the sins, Luther said, 'Now, with a red pen write over that list, The blood of Jesus Christ, God's Son, cleanses us from all sin.' The devil had nothing to say. Luther's reliance upon the ink of Holy Scripture (especially the 'red ink' revealed in the Bible) is one of his enduring legacies. The belief that the heart of each and every page of Scripture is the sacrificial blood of the Lamb is the touchstone of our own faith and the measuring stick by which we are called to evaluate what any Christian or Christian congregation believes, teaches and confesses." [3]

Satan knows how to shoot his flaming arrows at your vulnerable places. His arrows include, but are not limited to:

- **Anything to get you to disobey God.** Satan would love to break down your faith to the point where you lose faith in and disobey God. He knows that God's blessings and protection are related to obedience to Him (and he hates to see you blessed). Following are your solutions.
    - *Jesus replied, 'Anyone who loves Me will obey My teaching. My Father will love them, and We will come to them and make our home with them. Anyone who does not love Me will not obey My teaching. These words you hear are not My own; they belong to the Father who sent Me'* (John 14:23-24).
    - *Now all has been heard; here is the conclusion of the matter: Fear God and keep his commandments, for this is the duty of all mankind* (Ecclesiastes 12:13).
- **Blasphemous thoughts.** Thoughts like: "There is no God." "God does not love you." "God is not good." "Would a good God allow all this pain and suffering?" Remember, God delegated dominion over the earth to man, therefore whatever goes on here on earth is man's responsibility, not God's. God is good and He demonstrates His love for us. He will help man if he asks. See Genesis 1:28-30, Mark 10:18, Romans 5:8.
- **Critical and hateful thoughts** about yourself and others leading to breaking fellowship with God and man. *My command is this: Love each other as I have loved you* (John 15:12).
- **Thoughts of lust, wrath, revenge, or despair** which

3 From an article by Pastor Daniel Harmelink – Redeemer Lutheran Church, Huntington Beach, CA

Parker says are "capable of burning themselves deeply into your very souls, and all of them weakening your ability to resist whatever strategy he (Satan) plans next."

- **Sudden fears, anxieties, panic attacks, a dull feeling like nothing is right,** as in the case of King Saul in 1 Chronicles 10.
- **Medical attacks,** as in the case of Job.
- **Questioning the inspiration and authority of the Bible,** or its foundational principles: the deity of Christ, His atoning sacrifice on your behalf, or Salvation by grace, through faith in Christ **alone**.

THE SOURCE OF FAITH

"Faith in 'the shield of faith' means application of what we believe as an answer to everything that the devil hurls at us" (Martyn Lloyd Jones).

Of course our faith is in God, not the shield. The armor of God is a metaphor, a very strong mental image of the power of God and the different weaknesses and supernatural resources and solutions we have in our struggle *against the rulers, against the authorities, against the powers of this dark world, and against the spiritual forces of evil in the heavenly realms* (Ephesians 6:12).

Practically, this means that as the devil flings evil thoughts your way, we turn them back with a quick application of God's truth. If you feel your faith is weak, confess it to God and ask Him to increase your faith, as the father of the demoniac boy in Mark 9 did: *"I do believe; help me overcome my unbelief"* (Mark 9:24)!

Faith is a gift from God and therefore, one of the ways He keeps us from becoming prideful over what we do or have done. *Consequently, faith comes from hearing the message, and the message is heard through the word about Christ* (Romans 10:17).

As Christians, our life is intended to be a strategic partnership with God. He needs us to fulfill His purpose and plans summarized in The Great Commission (Matthew 28:19-20). We need Him to give us life to the fullest, teach us, guide us and protect us. As with any functional team, this strategic partnership requires a declaration of interdependence on each other. In this case, God has already made a declaration of interdependence on us. We are the Body of Christ, His implementers of The Great Commission and therefore, His only plan to get the job done. There is no back-up plan. His declaration of interdependence has been declared, so it is now only up to each of us to obey Christ and make a declaration of interdependence on Him!

STANDING FIRM AFTER PUTTING ON YOUR SHIELD OF FAITH

When Satan tries to persuade you to do things his way instead of God's way, remember that God is bound by His Promise, His way and His Word – He cannot lie or deviate from it. The promises He has made are irrevocable and the warnings He gives us are faithful and true.

Several years ago I noticed that the Old Testament tells us repeatedly to tell of God's glory and faithfulness throughout the earth. So I decided to openly thank Him at Christmas in our business newsletter, give Him credit for our success and quote Scripture to back it up. Honestly, I did this with some fear and concern as to the "political incorrectness" of the decision. But I decided that, when I stood before Christ on Judgment Day, He was going to be more concerned with the political correctness of the Kingdom's culture than the World's culture. So I proceeded.

Over the years I have received a number of comments about this practice from both Christians and non-Christians - some supportive, some not so supportive. Even some Christian business owners questioned whether it was appropriate. Every year, Satan would work on my mind and circumstances to try to stop me from publishing the letter. Every year I have chosen to do it anyway. What I can tell you is that the Lord has always taken care of me, my family and my business beyond what I could have imagined or deserved. Here is God's Word on the matter:

* *I will deliver this vast army into your hands, and you will know that I am the LORD* (1 Kings 20:28).
* *And without faith it is impossible to please God, because anyone who comes to Him must believe that He exists and that He rewards those who earnestly seek Him* (Hebrews 11:6).
* *But, seek first His kingdom and His righteousness, and all these things will be given to you* (Matthew 6:33).

Following is a brief Action Plan to improve your effective use of the Shield of Faith in winning the war against the spiritual forces of darkness:

1. **Read** the Bible regularly so the Holy Spirit can remind you of what Scripture says during Satan's attacks.
2. **Obey** Scripture in your daily life (Psalm 119:11, Deuteronomy 12:28).
3. **Allow** the Holy Spirit to sanctify you and counsel you (John 14:26 and Luke 12:12).
4. **Resist** the devil, and he will flee from you (James 4:7). Resist means to repel, defy, or thwart - not to agree with, not to receive his thoughts into your mind and soul and not to entertain anything that is contrary to the Word of God! Take comfort in the fact that your brothers and sisters in Christ are subject to the same learning process (1 Peter 5:8-9).
5. **Quote** Scripture back to Satan as Jesus did.

6. **Focus** on overcoming the World and Satan, (1 John 5:4-5).
7. **Unite** with other Christians. Make a declaration of interdependence with true believers and work together. Satan uses the age old strategy of "divide and conquer" (Ecclesiastes 4:9-12). Don't let him divide us.
8. **Practice trusting God daily** in your problem solving, decisions and actions by basing them only on Christ's teachings.
9. **Ask Christ to increase your faith.**

“EVERY TIME YOU AFFIRM
YOUR TRUST IN ME,
YOU PUT A COIN INTO MY TREASURY.
THUS YOU BUILD UP EQUITY
IN PREPARATION FOR DAYS OF TROUBLE.
I KEEP SAFELY IN MY HEART
ALL TRUST INVESTED IN ME,
WITH INTEREST COMPOUNDED CONTINUOUSLY.
THE MORE YOU TRUST ME,
THE MORE I EMPOWER YOU TO DO SO.”

Sarah Young, Jesus Calling

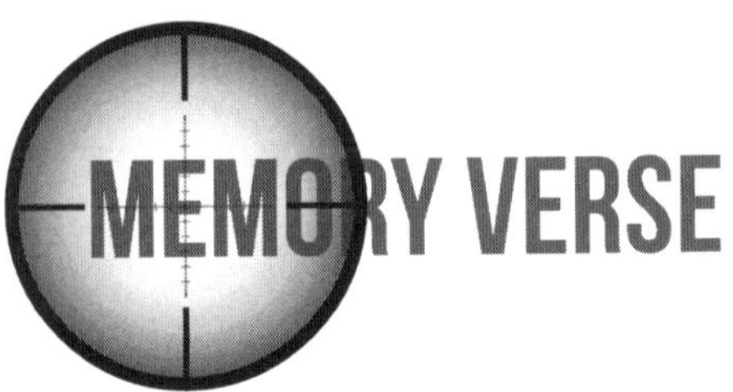

And without faith it is impossible to please God, because anyone who comes to Him must believe that He exists and that He rewards those who earnestly seek Him.

Hebrews 11:6

QUESTIONS FOR CONSIDERATION:

- What is the Shield of Faith? What are the five characteristics of the Shield of Faith?
- What are seven flaming arrows of the devil? How does he use them in your life and career or business?
- What is the source of faith?
- What is the currency of the Kingdom? How does it differ from the world's currencies? How does it impact your career or business?
- What is your action plan to use the Shield of Faith in your career or business?

We demolish arguments
and every pretension that sets itself up
against the knowledge of God,
and we take captive every thought to
make it obedient to Christ.
2 Corinthians 10:5
THE
HELMET
OF
SALVATION

CHAPTER 8

THE HELMET OF SALVATION

Putting on the Helmet of Salvation prevents Satan from derailing your spiritual growth with destructive thoughts. It allows you to experience the fruit of the Spirit, God's blessings and protection, and the honor of making disciples.

"The helmet of salvation protects the Christian from the devil's attacks on the mind. How we think will have a major impact on whether we can stand when the devil hurls his fiery darts. He can plant destructive thoughts in your mind in such a way that you fail to see their origin. Properly understood, the helmet of salvation prevents Satan from filling your mind with destructive thoughts" (Pastor Parker).

WHAT IS SALVATION?

Salvation should not be viewed as a "religious" concept. Salvation is a very practical and powerful event which provides a solution to man's sin condition, adoption into God's family and life everlasting, (Romans 3:22-23, John 1:12-13 and John 3:16). It also offers protection from Satan and the forces of evil and instruction in how to walk with the counsel of God's Spirit so you can live under God's favor (His blessing and supernatural intervention) resulting in what Christ called a full life. *The thief comes only to steal and kill and destroy; I came that they may have life, and have it to the full* (John 10:10).

To understand salvation, the subject must be broken down into components, each of which has very practical applications for providing us with both eternal life and life on earth in its fullness. There are five major components of salvation:

1. **Payment** for the penalty of disobeying God's law, leading to eternal life;
2. **Deliverance** from the body of sin by providing you with a new nature;
3. **Resources** to help you "Put off your old nature and put on your new nature";
4. **Membership** in God's family making you joint heirs with His Son, Jesus Christ, and citizenship in the Kingdom of God, a holy nation; and
5. **A new indestructible body** when you go to heaven, for your eternal life with God.

Numbers 4 and 5 have been covered already in previous chapters, so let's look at the first three elements a little closer:

1. **Payment for the penalty of disobeying God's law.** Salvation means to be delivered from something that intends you harm (for example, see Exodus 14:13). In the New Testament, salvation is generally used to refer to deliverance from the eternal penalty of sin and into

God's Kingdom. Our sins break God's laws, which are designed for our good. Sin requires the death penalty. God's justice requires that penalty. But God's loving mercy provided the most incredible substitute. Jesus Christ, our Creator Himself, was willing to die in our place! To be saved, we need a Savior.

What is the penalty of our sins, and how did God save us from that penalty? God answers this very plainly in His Word: *For the wages of sin is death, but the gift of God is eternal life in Christ Jesus our Lord* (Romans 6:23). But God demonstrates His own love for us in this: *While we were still sinners, Christ died for us* (Romans 5:8). *For God so loved the world that He gave His one and only Son, that whoever believes in Him shall not perish but have eternal life* (John 3:16). You learned in Chapter 1 how to receive forgiveness for your sins and obtain eternal life by putting your faith in Jesus Christ. This is what Real Christianity is founded on as reviewed in more detail in Chapter 1. It is referred to as **Imputed Righteousness,** the actual righteousness of Christ accredited to those who accept God's free gift of salvation through Christ's death on the cross. This is a one-time event in your life and, despite the fact that you may continue to sin, it NEVER changes. See Chapter 5 for more information on Imputed Righteousness.

2. **Deliverance from the "body of sin"** by providing you with a new nature - *Put off your old nature which belongs to your former manner of life and is corrupt through deceitful lusts, and be renewed in the spirit of your minds, and put on the new nature, created after the likeness of God in true righteousness and holiness* (Ephesians 4:22-24 RSV). This *new nature* is capable of functioning in "true righteousness and holiness" if the old sin nature remains "dead" (Romans 6) through daily faith in Christ. Learning to "put off your old nature" so it remains powerless is an ongoing salvation process Christians call sanctification. The Apostle Paul instructs us to *continue to work out your*

salvation with fear and trembling, for it is God who works in you to will and to act in order to fulfill His good purpose (Philippians 2:12-13). If we are saved by grace and not by works, why does Paul tell you to "work out your salvation"? There is a very important distinction in Paul's instructions here that can be very easily overlooked. This **Imparted Righteousness** (sanctification), is a process of learning how to live in your earthly body of sin through the power of the Holy Spirit living in you. As you walk by the Spirit (Galatians 5:16), Christ's righteousness is imparted to you to enable you to live righteously in your *new nature* through the power of Christ in you. This is a process and it will continue while you are on earth. See Chapter 5 for more information on imparted righteousness.

3. **Resources to help you put off your old nature and put on your new nature.** To help you with the sanctification process, you have four very powerful supernatural resources:

   » Christ in you (Galatians 4:6),

   » The Holy Spirit counseling you (John 16:13),

   » Scripture, providing you with the Word of God (Psalm 119:105) and

   » Angels ministering to you (Hebrews 1:14).

   The concept that we are both saved and being sanctified at the same time may be confusing to you as it was to me at one time. Hebrews 10:14 sheds some light on this seeming contradiction, *For by one sacrifice He has made perfect forever those who are being made holy.* In order to receive your sanctification, you must cooperate with the Holy Spirit every day because only God can make you godly.

The Apostle Paul confirms this for us: *I planted the seed, Apollos watered it, but God has been making it grow. So neither the one who plants nor the one who waters is anything, but only God, who makes things grow* (1 Corinthians 3:5-8).

Our responsibility in the process is to believe in God the Father and the Lord Jesus Christ and cooperate with Him by doing what He instructs us to do in the Bible, His "operating manual" for life on earth. Jesus answered, *"The work of God is this: to believe in the One He has sent"* (John 6:29).

SATAN'S SCHEMES TO DERAIL YOUR SANCTIFICATION PROCESS

Nothing is more dangerous to Satan's schemes than a Christian who knows his position in Christ and understands the Word of God and how to use it. That's why salvation is symbolized as a helmet, because it protects your mind. Not only should our way of life be different from the world, but our way of thinking should too. We have been called out of this world, metaphorically speaking, and, though we live in it, we should live separate from it.

Paul calls us to be transformed by the renewing of your mind (Romans 12:2). This involves having God's Word in your minds and meditating on it so you can better follow it (Hebrews 10:16; Psalm 119:11). In this way, God gives us the ability to obey His commandments through His power, not ours.

Satan hates that we have chosen this path and will stop at nothing to keep us from completing it. Just as the helmet protects the vital but vulnerable head from otherwise fatal blows, the hope of salvation can protect our thoughts from our enemy's attacks and temptations to disobey God. He will attack your weaknesses, getting you to indulge tempting thoughts until you can no longer resist and you act on them. *Be alert and of sober mind. Your enemy the devil prowls around like a roaring lion looking for someone to devour. Resist him, standing firm in the faith, because you know that the family of believers throughout the world is undergoing the same kind of sufferings*

(1 Peter 5:8-9). You resist him by dismissing the thoughts from your mind *(taking them captive)* and not indulging them to the point they overwhelm you with a desire to act on them. Then quote a scripture to Satan, such as *I can do all things through Christ who strengthens me* (Philippians 4:13 NKJV).

Without the helmet of salvation, we will be unprotected from the cares of this world that bombard our thoughts and feelings. Imagine not knowing what the future ultimately holds. The worries and problems produced by living in this world would overwhelm us! *For everyone born of God overcomes the world. This is the victory that has overcome the world, even our faith* (1 John 5:4).

With the helmet securely fastened, we can have the same confidence that Paul did that a better future lies ahead of us: *our present sufferings are not worth comparing with the glory that will be revealed in us* (Romans 8:18).

PUTTING ON THE HELMET OF SALVATION

"On the crest and other parts of the Roman helmet were a great variety of emblematic figures. It is believed that the Roman soldiers had special ceremonial helmets, worn during parades, that denoted their rank. When Paul refers to the helmet of salvation, it is very likely the apostle refers to helmets which had on them an emblem that signified the hope of the soldier who wore it, that he would be safe in battle and prosperous in all his engagements. Likewise, donning the helmet of salvation, through the blood of the Lamb, gives us hope to conquer every adversary, surmount every difficulty and enjoy continuous safety and protection as our divine right. This protection extends to the workings of our mind, blocking attacks of darkness and confusion by any temptations of Satan. By carrying Christ in our hearts, we cannot be cheated out of the hope of Heaven"

(From Adam Clarke's Commentary).

Pastor Parker describes the Helmet's protection this way: "If you know you are saved, if you know you belong to God and He belongs to you, if you know that all God's promises are sealed in the blood of His Son, it is very hard for the devil to knock you down. Moreover, if in being saved you have learned to look forward to Heaven as your true home, if your desire for God and Heaven has reached the point that you will settle for nothing less, you will stand like a rock…The man or woman who wears the helmet of salvation will stand in the fight against the devil because his hopes are too high, too big to be satisfied on this earth. His mind is set on heavenly things, not on earthly things."

Does this mean that you and your process have to be perfect? Abraham is cited in Hebrews as the model example of faith in God, yet he "failed" in the process several times that we know of, losing faith and taking matters into his own hands, having his offspring with a concubine. Twice he lied about Sarah to men who wanted her. But in the end, Abraham kept his focus on Heaven, despite the setbacks along the way and was rewarded by God for his faith, demonstrated by obedience.

Again, Pastor Parker: "Abraham stayed faithful to God because he had something in mind beyond the confines of this world. The writer of Hebrews tells us that Abraham knew that God had promised him a heavenly home - a permanent, heavenly city with eternal foundations. That's the vision that kept Abraham faithful. That's why all his life he refused to settle down and build something permanent…His tent was itself a confession of his heart's desire. Like the old gospel song says, he was telling the world – 'This world is not my home, I'm just passing through, my treasures are laid up, somewhere beyond the blue.'"

The confession of a believer's heart is different for each person. What is your confession of your heart's desire for Heaven? The hope of Heaven – that vision of the city with foundations – will keep you standing when there's no earthly reason to do so!

SATAN'S SCHEMES TO KNOCK YOUR HELMET OFF

Following are five strategies Satan will use to work on your mind to create confusion and disbelief:

- **Satan will strive to get you to give up.** This may include things like: stop going to church, stop giving to God's work, stop spending time with God in His Word and/or in prayer, stop focusing on living in your new nature instead of your old nature, not staying on the narrow path, not providing services for the Kingdom, not believing in your victory over sin and Satan, not obeying God or not believing in God's promises.
- **Satan will try to get you to join his side.** This can be done by just quitting, joining a religion other than Christianity, making this present world more important than God's Kingdom, or attending a Christian church that embraces an empty, watered-down theology that does not adhere to Scripture.
- **Satan will subtly persuade you to embrace his point of view.** In doing so he will work on your mind until you agree with him in such beliefs as:
    - This world is all there is,
    - This life is all that has meaning,
    - Material things matter most ("he who dies with the most toys wins"),
    - I will pursue whatever feels good and gives me pleasure,
    - Power is the way to get what you want,
    - The end justifies the means,

- Sex outside of marriage is acceptable,
- God is not personally involved in my day-to-day life, etc.

- **One of the most destructive of Satan's lies** in today's world may be "Abortion does not result in killing a human being because an unborn baby is just a mass of tissue." Is that what the advocates of that lie are going to tell Christ when they stand before Him? Perhaps they should more deeply consider King David's prayer to God in Psalm 139, ***For You created my inmost being; You knit me together in my mother's womb.*** *I praise You because I am fearfully and wonderfully made; Your works are wonderful, I know that full well. My frame was not hidden from You when I was made in the secret place, when I was woven together in the depths of the earth. Your eyes saw my unformed body; all the days ordained for me were written in Your book before one of them came to be* (Psalm 139:13-16).
- **Satan will subtly get you to become his agent without you even knowing it.** "Misery loves company." This is one of his worst strategies and includes things such as:
  - Influencing other Christians to buy-in to one or more of the first four above,
  - Introducing friends or family to pornography, infidelity or other sexual sins,
  - Influencing others to distrust God, or
  - Destroying God's work through gossip, pervasive negativity, anger, constant criticism, distracting others from their Kingdom work, etc.
- **Satan will try to get you to give up on God by getting you to believe the rewards are not worth the cost.** He does this through such thoughts as: "God doesn't really care about me," "Heaven is no big deal," "Who wants to just lie around and worship God every day," or "God is not a good God, why would He let this happen to me?"

Or others.

- **Satan will persuade you to function in your dysfunction.** In other words, Satan wants to destroy our hope. The Apostle Paul instructs us concerning the matter of hope:
    - *Not only so, but we also glory in our sufferings, because we know that suffering produces perseverance; perseverance, character; and character, hope. And hope does not put us to shame, because God's love has been poured out into our hearts through the Holy Spirit, who has been given to us* (Romans 5:3-5).
    - *May the God of hope fill you with all joy and peace as you trust in him, so that you may overflow with hope by the power of the Holy Spirit* (Romans 15:13).

These two Scriptures hold the secret to preventing Satan from being successful in filling your mind with destructive thoughts. If you set your mind on what the Spirit desires, your hope is in a "full life" with Christ as your Lord. Focused on eternal life with Him in the Kingdom, there will be no place for Satan's attacks on your mind and emotions.

FIVE STRATEGIES FOR USING THE HELMET OF SALVATION

Our Heavenly Father does not want us being satisfied to function in our dysfunction. He sent His Son so we might experience life in its fullness by functioning in our *new nature* which is not dysfunctional. This is made possible by Christ rendering our *old sin nature* powerless as we put our trust in Him daily.

Following are five strategies the Bible provides on how to use the Helmet of Salvation to strongly defend yourself during your struggles with Satan and his forces of evil. You are using the Helmet of Salvation when:

» **You want to go to Heaven because it's more**

fascinating, important and valuable than any place on this earth, so you have set your mind on it until your affections for Heaven are greater than your affections for this world. This will happen when you understand that:

* Your real Father and family are located there,
* Your ultimate spiritual and emotional desires will be satisfied there and only there,
* Real rewards will be distributed there and only there,
* Your work for the Kingdom will not be in vain. Your work (effort) for the Kingdom (including a calling by God to work in business) will last forever, and Heaven has the greatest "cost-benefit" relationship. In other words, to the degree we give our lives and our wealth to things that will be permanent and provide everlasting returns, we will, to the same degree, desire Heaven.

» **You give your loyalty to Christ and the Kingdom. You exercise this loyalty when:**

* You obey God,
* You obey Christ's teachings,
* You stand up with Christ and defend Him,
* You live according to the principles of the Kingdom Culture, not the world's culture and
* You declare God's glory and faithfulness throughout the earth (Psalm 96:3, Psalm 40:10). *Because, You are a chosen people, a royal priesthood, a holy nation, God's special possession, that you may declare the praises of Him who called you out of darkness into His wonderful light. Once you were not a people, but now you are the people of God* (1 Peter 2:9-10).

» **Your life is ruled by Kingdom principles.**

* **Growth in holiness and Christ-likeness is not a means to salvation, it is proof of salvation.** In other words, we are not saved because we are holy, we

are holy and can live a godly life because we are saved. *Dear children, do not let anyone lead you astray. The one who does what is right is righteous, just as He is righteous. This is how we know who the children of God are and who the children of the devil are: Anyone who does not do what is right is not God's child, nor is anyone who does not love their brother and sister* (1 John 3:7, 10).

* **When we realize the abundant grace that caused Christ to go to the Cross for us, we will be drawn to a holy life.** *All who have this hope in Him purify themselves, just as He is pure* (1 John 3:3). The benefit? We share in Christ's glory: *But we ought always to thank God for you, brothers and sisters loved by the Lord, because God chose you as first fruits to be saved through the sanctifying work of the Spirit and through belief in the truth. He called you to this through our gospel, that you might share in the glory of our Lord Jesus Christ. So then, brothers and sisters, stand firm and hold fast to the teachings we passed on to you, whether by word of mouth or by letter* (2 Thessalonians 2:13-15).

» **You do what you can to build up those who are in the faith.**

* *From Him the whole body, joined and held together by every supporting ligament, grows and builds itself up in love, as each part does its work* (Ephesians 4:16).
* *Let us hold unswervingly to the hope we profess, for He who promised is faithful. And let us consider how we may spur one another on toward love and good deeds, not give up meeting together, as some are in the habit of doing, but encouraging one another — and all the more as you see the Day approaching* (Hebrews 10:23-25).

» **You stand with Jesus (your King) and those who stand with Him.**

* *Whoever acknowledges Me before others, I will also acknowledge him before my Father in Heaven. But*

whoever disowns Me before others, I will disown him before my Father in Heaven (Matthew 10:32-33).

* *We ought always to thank God for you, brothers and sisters, and rightly so, because your faith is growing more and more, and the love all of you have for one another is increasing. Therefore, among God's churches we boast about your perseverance and faith in all the persecutions and trials you are enduring* (2 Thessalonians 1:3-4).

This is the salvation you are fighting for—living under the power, protection, and blessings of the Kingdom of God while on earth to give you victory over the flesh (the old nature), the world and Satan! And, someday participating in the coming rule of the Kingdom of God on earth and living in the heavenly Kingdom, with its beauty, love, peace and rewards for eternity! That's what makes the battles in this life worth it and that's what helps you keep your eye on the goal.

Then I saw "a new heaven and a new earth," for the first heaven and the first earth had passed away, and there was no longer any sea. I saw the Holy City, the new Jerusalem, coming down out of heaven from God, prepared as a bride beautifully dressed for her husband. And I heard a loud voice from the throne saying, "Look! God's dwelling place is now among the people, and He will dwell with them. They will be His people, and God Himself will be with them and be their God. 'He will wipe every tear from their eyes. There will be no more death' or mourning or crying or pain, for the old order of things has passed away (Revelation 21:1-4).

STANDING FIRM AFTER PUTTING ON YOUR HELMET OF SALVATION

When the devil tempted Christ in Luke 4:1-13, Christ ALWAYS used Scripture, and ONLY Scripture, to take His stand against him. Because He knew that God is much more powerful than Satan and that Scripture has divine power to demolish strongholds, Jesus took captive every thought that Satan threw at Him that was contrary to Scripture. Satan tried to tempt and manipulate Him and Jesus simply rejected it, not letting it take root in His mind. He stood His ground with only Scripture as His weapon!

Christ knew Satan fears God the Father and that if He stood on the truth of God's word, Satan would give up and go away. *When the devil had finished all this tempting, he left Him until an opportune time* (Luke 4:13). "Is that it?" you ask. "Is that all I have to do?" Yes, that's all there is and that's all you have to do! Do not battle with people. Do not battle with your flesh. Just quote Scripture to Satan, believe the Scripture and then trust in God's power. *I will deliver this vast army into your hands, and you will know that I am the LORD* (1 Kings 20:28).

Three final reminders:

Be patient with yourself and others. *For we know that our old self was crucified with Him so that the body ruled by sin might be done away with, that we should no longer be slaves to sin— because anyone who has died has been set free from sin. Now if we died with Christ, we believe that we will also live with Him* (Romans 6:6-8).

To succeed in sanctification, rely on the power of Christ living in you. *I have been crucified with Christ and I no longer live, but Christ lives in me. The life I now live in the body, I live by faith in the Son of God, who loved me and gave Himself for me. I do not set aside the grace of God, for if righteousness could be gained through the law, Christ died for nothing* (Galatians 2:20-21)!

In the words of Winston Churchill "Never, never, never give up!" *Stand firm and you will see the deliverance the Lord will bring you today* (Exodus 14:13).

MY DEAR CHILDREN,

I WRITE THIS TO YOU SO THAT YOU WILL NOT SIN.
BUT IF ANYBODY DOES SIN,
WE HAVE AN ADVOCATE WITH THE FATHER —
JESUS CHRIST, THE RIGHTEOUS ONE.
HE IS THE ATONING SACRIFICE FOR OUR SINS,
AND NOT ONLY FOR OURS
BUT ALSO FOR THE SINS OF THE WHOLE WORLD.

The Apostle John

No, in all these things we are more than conquerors through Him Who loved us. For I am convinced that neither death nor life, neither angels nor demons, neither the present nor the future, nor any powers, neither height nor depth, nor anything else in all creation, will be able to separate us from the love of God that is in Christ Jesus our Lord.

Romans 8:37-39

QUESTIONS FOR CONSIDERATION:

- What is the Helmet of Salvation?
- What are the different components of salvation?
- What schemes is Satan using to derail your salvation? How do they affect your life and career or business?
- What are five strategies for using the Helmet? How can they improve your career or business?
- What is your action plan to use the Helmet?

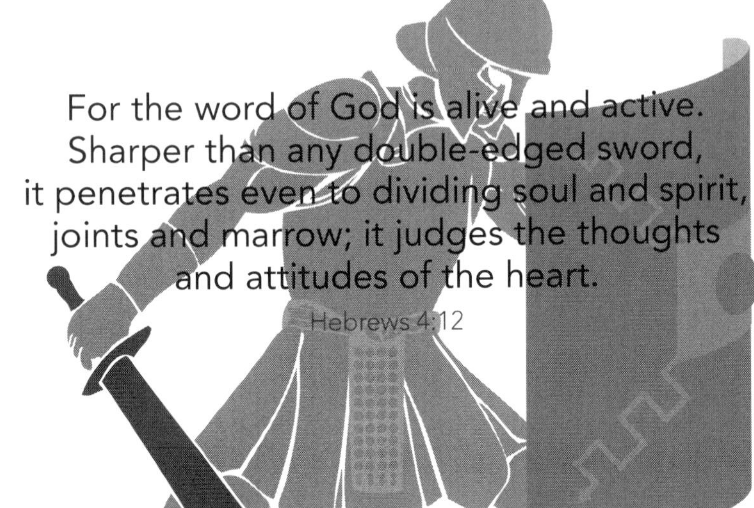

For the word of God is alive and active.
Sharper than any double-edged sword,
it penetrates even to dividing soul and spirit,
joints and marrow; it judges the thoughts
and attitudes of the heart.

Hebrews 4:12

THE SWORD OF THE SPIRIT

CHAPTER 9

THE SWORD OF THE SPIRIT

So far, we have mostly utilized defensive pieces of armor – belt, shoes...In this chapter, we're going to look at an offensive piece: the Sword of the Spirit. Other pieces of armor offer us comfort, knowing that we can rely on the protection that they offer us. But seen as a Sword, Scripture enables us to not only stand against Satan, but to actively put him to flight.

PUTTING ON THE SWORD OF THE SPIRIT

The Roman *gladius* was most likely the sword that Paul had in mind when he wrote the book of Ephesians. Known as "the sword that conquered the world," the *gladius* was adapted from a Spanish design and was unique in that it had two sharpened edges and a hard, tapered point that could pierce through heavy armor. Certainly a formidable weapon in its day!

The Word of God is Truth – pure, unadulterated Truth,

plain and simple. It is light, illuminating for us the good and the bad, so we can eliminate confusion, define reality and make wiser choices for our lives. *Your word is a lamp for my feet, a light on my path* (Psalm 119:105). With this light, we do not need to stumble around in darkness. We have a true and unerring guide for the paths that we need to walk. Lack of knowledge of the Word can lead to our destruction (Hosea 4:6), but hearing and keeping the Word will surely lead to our being blessed (Luke 11:28).

Why compare the Word to a sword? Just as the powerful Roman sword cut through the enemy's armor, the truth of the Word can cut through the defenses of our enemy and the confusion in your mind and heart. For the word of God is alive and active. *Sharper than any double-edged sword, it penetrates even to dividing soul and spirit, joints and marrow; it judges the thoughts and attitudes of the heart* (Hebrews 4:12). The Sword of Truth, when wielded by a believer, cuts straight to the core of any matter and uncovers the truth of the situation. It is the responsibility and the duty of every soldier in God's army to use the Sword to discern truth and follow it. Jesus Himself used the Sword of the Word when He fended off Satan's attacks in the desert (Matthew 4:4, 7, 10).

We can even use the Sword to perform spiritual battlefield surgery when we discover lies and wrong beliefs in our own thoughts and actions as well as that of others as the Apostle Paul instructs us in 2 Corinthians 10:3-5: *For though we live in the world, we do not wage war as the world does. On the contrary, they have divine power to demolish strongholds. We demolish arguments and every pretension that sets itself up against the knowledge of God, and we take captive every thought to make it obedient to Christ.*

Finally, since the Sword is the only offensive weapon mentioned in Paul's description of the armor of God, this would seem to imply to us that close-range combat is going to be the nature of our battles. Otherwise, Paul might have talked about the "Longbow of the Lord." We apparently don't need to concern ourselves with the enemy's movements on the other side of the battlefield. That's for someone else to fight. Our Sword is sufficient for our defense and our offense. Armed with our Sword, emboldened by the Spirit, we face our enemy head-on. No powers of hell can stand against the Word of God in the hands of a trained warrior! *If God is for us, who can be against us* (Romans 8:31)?

THE POWER OF YOUR OFFENSIVE WEAPON

As a born again Christian, do you now know deep in your heart who the Bible says you are? If not, I recommend you spend more time meditating on this amazing truth. The Apostle John expresses this wonder in 1 John 3:1, *See what great love the Father has lavished on us, that we should be called children of God! And that is what we are!* The Apostle Peter deepens the meaning for us, *you are a chosen people, a royal priesthood, a holy nation, a people belonging to God* (1 Peter 2:9). Collectively, true Christians are a holy nation, that is, we all belong to one nation, the Kingdom of God, and we are citizens of that nation, with all the rights of a citizen and the protection of its King!

Since you are a citizen of God's Kingdom, you are a natural enemy of Satan and his forces of darkness and therefore, a soldier while on earth. As we saw earlier in the book, there is a cosmic war going on in heaven and on earth, a war for the restoration of mankind and rule over the planet. Therefore, Christians must put on our spiritual armor and gird on our swords for fighting. In Heaven we will be the Church Triumphant, or the church at rest, but now, in this life we are the Church Militant. Christ has won the Kingdom's presence on earth for us, but He is waiting for us to go out in faith to advance that Kingdom. That means that in this life every born-again child of God is a soldier, from the youngest, sweetest little seven-year-old girl who just invited Jesus to come live in her heart, to the oldest, weakest little grandmother who can't even get out of bed without assistance. [1]

To fight this war effectively, with skill and confidence you must first know and understand your identity as a child of God and a citizen of the Kingdom of God! To live in the fullness of life Christ came to provide, you must come to a deep understanding that you are using your power or strength to battle Satan, not people. Christ commanded us to love people. And The Promise is conditional on your compliance with His commands.

As Christian soldiers bearing the Word of God, empowered by His Spirit, we carry devastating firepower! Every Christian has the potential to be a dangerous and powerful opponent to the spiritual forces of the devil. When we win a battle, angels rejoice. When Satan loses a soul to the Kingdom of God, that lost soul (lost to him that is) becomes a found soul to God and a winner in the spiritual realm.

We are called to be soldiers who will march into the devil's prisoner of war camps and set them free! Knowing our weapon, the Sword of the Spirit, enables us to do that. Most importantly, unless you understand how to win the war with Satan, you are easy prey for him and his forces of darkness.

---

1 Thanks to Pastor Shafer Parker for this concept.

FIVE WAYS GOD'S SPIRIT AIDS YOU IN USING THE SWORD

The Holy Spirit guides you into all truth (John 16:13) and thus, helps you to understand and use the Sword:

1. **The Holy Spirit inspired men to write Scripture for you.** Part of His plan in doing so was to equip God's children with truth to counter every one of the devil's attacks. *Above all, you must understand that no prophecy of Scripture came about by the prophet's own interpretation of things. For prophecy never had its origin in the human will, but prophets, though human, spoke from God as they were carried along by the Holy Spirit* (2 Peter 1:20-21). Read Scripture on a regular basis!
2. **The Holy Spirit leads us** in our understanding of reality and anything we need to know. *When He, the Spirit of truth, comes, He will guide you into all the truth. He will not speak on His own; He will speak only what He hears, and He will tell you what is yet to come. He will glorify me because it is from Me that He will receive what He will make known to you. All that belongs to the Father is mine. That is why I said the Spirit will receive from Me what He will make known to you* (John 16:13-15). Also read Colossians 1:9 and 2:2-4, as well as Romans 10:17. Seek His counsel, teaching and training!
3. **The Holy Spirit enables us to understand Scripture.** *However, as it is written: "What no eye has seen, what no ear has heard, and what no human mind has conceived"- the things God has prepared for those who love Him— these are the things God has revealed to us by His Spirit. The Spirit searches all things, even the deep things of God. For who knows a person's thoughts except their own spirit within them? In the same way no one knows the thoughts of God except the Spirit of God. What we have received is not the spirit of the world, but the Spirit who is from God, so that we may understand what God has freely given us. This is what we speak, not in words taught us by human wisdom but in words taught by the Spirit, explaining spiritual realities*

with Spirit-taught words (1 Corinthians 2:9-13). Ask for and seek understanding of Scripture and how to apply it!

4. **The Holy Spirit reminds us of appropriate passages in Scripture in times of need.** *But the Advocate, the Holy Spirit, whom the Father will send in My name, will teach you all things and will remind you of everything I have said to you* (John 14:26). *Do not worry about what to say or how to say it. At that time you will be given what to say, for it will not be you speaking, but the Spirit of your Father speaking through you* (Matthew 10:19-20). Memorize Scripture, the best you can! Personally, I don't have a good memory, but I do the best I can.
5. **The Holy Spirit empowers the Word as it is spoken** to accomplish His intended effect on you and your calling as well as that of people under your influence. *All Scripture is God-breathed and is useful for teaching, rebuking, correcting and training in righteousness, so that the servant of God may be thoroughly equipped for every good work* (2 Timothy 3:16-17). Speak and live Scripture out in your life, especially in the world. You do not need to quote verses precisely. **Just speaking the Word of God in your natural words will reap the benefits Paul is describing here.**

KEEPING YOUR SWORD SHARP!

A dull weapon is an ineffective weapon! Keep your sword sharp to assist in your battles with the enemy:

1. **Know what the Bible says well enough to know where it says it.** This doesn't mean you have to memorize huge blocks of Scripture, but it does mean that reading God's word should be such a regular practice for you that you know the general location of scriptural concepts and stories. The more you are able to do this, the more the Holy Spirit can teach you and remind you of truth when you need it.

2. **"Use it or lose it"** as the old saying goes. Like anything else you want to learn, it is not enough to just read the Bible. In order to understand what it means and how it works, you have to apply it in your daily decisions and actions. It is by applying what you learn that you develop divine judgment and accelerate your sanctification. Through practice, you develop discernment in knowing Christ's voice from the voice of Satan and any other voices that may have been programmed in your mind throughout your life. *You also develop judgment like the sons of Issachar, who understood the times and knew what Israel should do* (1 Chronicles 12:32). That is, knowing which spiritual principle of truth to apply in each specific life situation.
3. **Pray for grace to love God's Word.** The Word should matter to you more than anything else, even life itself. God's Word provides you with wisdom for life! *Man does not live on bread alone but on every word that comes from the mouth of the LORD* (Deuteronomy 8:3). Jesus quoted this Scripture to Satan during His temptation because He understood that the Word of God is powerful and that obeying it produces real life and the blessings of God. *The decrees of the Lord are firm, and all of them are righteous. They are more precious than gold, than much pure gold; they are sweeter than honey, than honey from the honeycomb. By them your servant is warned; in keeping them there is great reward* (Psalms 19:9-11).
4. **Be filled with the Spirit.** If you have set your mind on what He desires and are making a sincere effort in obeying Christ, the Holy Spirit will fill you with His presence and give you wisdom in your words and your actions. Read the

> book of Acts and see that those early disciples who turned the world upside down were filled with the Spirit, over and over. The Holy Spirit was the source of their - and our - power.

There are many similarities between the fifth chapter of Paul's letter to the Ephesians and the third chapter of his letter to the Colossians. The only fundamental difference between the two is that one instructs you to be filled with the Spirit and the other instructs you to *Let the Word of Christ dwell in you richly.* In other words, setting your *mind on what the Spirit desires* and basing your thoughts and actions on God's Word will produce the filling of the Spirit in your lives.

USING YOUR SWORD TO STOP BEING A VICTIM

In the early 1980's, I met periodically with a friend named Dave. We often discussed a number of different topics about life and Christianity. In one of our discussions I told him that after almost 25 years of being a Christian I was convinced that many church denominations, pastors and teachers didn't really trust the people in the pews to understand the Bible on their own and to make their own decisions, resulting in a dependent, legalistic culture (full of rules and regulations to tell people how to think and act). Dave was a graduate of Denver Seminary with a master's degree in counseling. He thought for a moment and then said "So, what you are saying is that many church denominations, pastors and teachers are neurotic parents." When I asked him for clarification, he responded, "Parents who are afraid to let their children grow up."

God wants each of His children to grow up spiritual and He gave us the freedom to do it. He gives us the grace and mercy as we stumble along the way (1John 1:9). Therefore do not be afraid, living as though you need any one person or denomination to achieve wisdom and godliness. Although we are to listen and learn from human teachers and counselors, Christ is our "Teacher." And the Holy Spirit our "Counselor" and Guide to the truth. Preachers and teachers of the gospel, including me, are only imperfect instruments in His service. As you can tell by all the different denominations and opinions of the truth in Christianity, you would be wise to rely primarily on One Shepherd who came to give us The Truth:

» *The words of the wise are like goads, their collected sayings like firmly embedded nails—given by one shepherd. Be warned, my son, of anything in addition to them. Of making many books there is no end, and much study wearies the body* (Ecclesiastes 12:11-12).

» *Jesus answered, "You say that I am a king. In fact, the reason I was born and came into the world is to testify to the truth. Everyone on the side of truth listens to Me"* (John 18:37).

First and foremost, read the Bible! Read it like I once heard Frances Shaeffer say he did. "I read it like any other book – like it means what it says. And when I was done, I believed it."

I once attended a most interesting workshop as part of a continuing education course. It was called *Management by Responsibility.* The workshop turned out to be far different from what the students were expecting. The premise of the training was that in every business there is at least one melodrama going on. They explained that, like all melodramas, the melodramas in each business are complete with people playing the roles of victim, persecutor and rescuer. These melodramas create dysfunctional behavior, bad decisions, inefficiencies and a lack of teamwork. Therefore, they have a significant negative impact on the success of the company and each participant in the melodrama. "All of these roles in the melodrama represent irresponsible behaviors," they declared. "The solution is for every participant in the melodrama to stop their irresponsible behavior and take 100% responsibility for their choices, decisions and behavior." Christians can learn a lot from management concepts, many of which come from Biblical principles. Christianity is a gigantic melodrama with millions of Christians willingly playing the role of victims. But in fact, the ultimate victim is Satan - and Christ has already won the battle with him. Once each Christian sees this clearly and understands who they are in Christ, they stop playing the role of the victim and take 100% responsibly for their choices, decisions and behavior.

True Christians are not victims; we are the children of God, and Christ, our King has already defeated Satan. That is why we rely on His Word! And having disarmed the powers and authorities, He made a public spectacle of them, triumphing over them by the cross (Colossians 2:15). When Satan comes to kill us, steal our inheritance and destroy our lives, our recourse is to walk as Jesus walked. When the devil came after Christ, the only begotten Son of God, He showed us the way. Christ ALWAYS used Scripture, and ONLY Scripture, to take His stand against the devil's schemes and put him on the run. Scripture is the Word of God, and Satan is afraid of God! You believe that there is one God. Good! Even the demons believe that—and shudder (James 2:19).

Do not allow yourself to be a persecutor or victim! Do not battle with people! Do not battle with your flesh! Love people and obey God as you quote Scripture to Satan, believing God's Word and trusting in God's power and promise, *I will deliver this vast army into your hands, and you will know that I am the LORD* (1 Kings 20:28).

With our Scriptural armor and weapon, the King of God's Kingdom as your leader and ally, the Holy Spirit as your Teacher and Counselor, and angels to minister to you; you can and <u>will</u> overcome the enemy!

In closing this chapter, let's review the Action Plan covered in Chapter 7. This will help you to be equipped and increase your effectiveness in your spiritual growth:

1. **Read** the Bible regularly so the Holy Spirit can remind you of what Scripture says.
2. **Obey** Scripture in your daily life (Psalm 119:11, Deuteronomy 12:28).
3. **Allow** the Holy Spirit to sanctify you and counsel you (John 14:26 and Luke 12:12).
4. **Resist** *the devil, and he will flee from you* (James 4:7). Resist means to repel, defy, or thwart - not to agree with, not to receive his thoughts into your mind and soul and not to entertain anything that is contrary to the Word of God! Take comfort in the fact that your brothers and sisters in Christ are subject to the same learning process (1 Peter 5:8-9).
5. **Quote** Scripture back to Satan as Jesus did. Memorize a few key verses for this purpose, such as 1 John 5:11-13, 1 John 1:9, Galatians 2:20-21, John 15:9-12, and others as the Holy Spirit instructs you to.
6. **Focus** on overcoming the World and Satan (1 John 5:4-5).
7. **Unite** with other Christians. Make a declaration of interdependence with true believers and work together. Satan uses the age old strategy of "divide and conquer," (Ecclesiastes 4:9-12). Don't let him divide you.
8. **Practice Trusting God Daily** in your daily problem solving, decisions and actions.

9. **Ask Christ to increase your faith.**
10. **Believe.** *Love the Lord your God with all your heart and with all your soul and with all your mind* (Matthew 22:37).

FOR THE WORD OF GOD IS
ALIVE AND ACTIVE.
SHARPER THAN ANY DOUBLE-EDGED SWORD,
IT PENETRATES EVEN TO DIVIDING SOUL AND SPIRIT,
JOINTS AND MARROW;
IT JUDGES THE THOUGHTS
AND ATTITUDES OF THE HEART.

Hebrews 4:12

The weapons we fight with are not the weapons of the world. On the contrary, they have divine power to demolish strongholds. We demolish arguments and every pretension that sets itself up against the knowledge of God, and we take captive every thought to make it obedient to Christ.

2 Corinthians 10:4-5

QUESTIONS FOR CONSIDERATION:

- What is the Sword of the Spirit?
- How is it different from the other pieces of armor?
- What are five ways to use the sword? How can you use them in your career or business?
- What are four ways to sharpen your sword?
- How can you use the sword currently in your life to overcome Satan? How can you put him on the run?

This is the confidence we have in approaching God: that if we ask anything according to His will, He hears us. And if we know that He hears us — whatever we ask — we know that we have what we asked of Him.

1 John 5:14-15

PRAYING IN THE SPIRIT

CHAPTER 10

PRAYING IN THE SPIRIT

I was having breakfast with the senior teaching pastor in our church in 1985 - at a time when I was processing some very painful damaged emotions from childhood. The pastor was also a good friend of mine, so we were accustomed to being very open with each other. Our discussion moved to prayer. Someone had recently told me she prayed for a parking spot and God had provided her with one. I told the pastor I couldn't even remotely identify with something so trivial. I had been hurting inside for months, asking God to heal the pain, with little or no improvement. My friend was also dealing with some very difficult medical issues with one of his children and he agreed he had a hard time understanding or even believing that God is involved in such minor details of our lives.

Since that time, the Lord has taught me that He is indeed interested in all the details of our life – both great and small - and taught me some key principles about living life on earth in our body of sin and seeing our prayers answered. God works through the natural principles, laws, methods and systems that He has built into His creation. I've put together a list of some key principles that I have learned from nearly six decades of following God:

God has established perpetual principles (the Ten Commandments) of how to relate to one another and to Him. He also instructed us that if we obey them, there are benefits and if we violate them, there are consequences. We were created with a soul (often referred to in Scripture as our "heart") that contains our emotions. When they are damaged (and all are damaged from time to time), there is a process we have to go through to restore our soul: *This is what the Lord says: "If you repent, I will restore you that you may serve Me"* (Jeremiah 15:19). Christians often lack understanding about this process and therefore expect other Christians, who have been hurt or damaged, to just "get over it and move on" without helping them through the natural process that is necessary to restore the soul.

People often wait until a huge crisis affects them personally (such as cancer or a broken relationship) before getting serious about building a mutual trust relationship with God. This relationship is best built by regularly praying about smaller things. This provides us with a clear understanding of His ways, His love for us and His wisdom on how to walk in His power day-by-day. A speaker taught me a very important lesson years ago. "Christians would be better off building their faith, their relationship with God, their trust in God and God's trust in them by asking Him for supernatural help and judgment in handling the small challenges and illnesses in life before asking Him to use His supernatural power for major issues like healing them of cancer!" Not that it's more difficult for God to heal cancer – but a regular regimen of seeing answered prayer builds up our faith, so that we can ask for major things and believe we will receive them.

Most people, including Christians, challenge God by their words or choices, concerning why He does what He does in their lives, the lives of others and the world at large. Challenging God can often be as simple as not obeying Him.

The Bible makes it clear in Job and Romans that God made us and that His intelligence and wisdom is vastly greater than ours. Therefore, we are foolish questioning His judgment, His testing, His decisions or His reprimands. As the song says, "Trust and Obey for There is No Other Way to be Happy in Jesus." No other way!

God deeply loves us and wants us to learn to walk in His ways and communicate with Him on a continual basis so He can teach us and bless us far beyond our imagination so we can fulfill His purposes. Therefore, sometimes, He defers answers to our prayers until we learn to do this.

Satan, our enemy, does not want us to discover these truths about God and about ourselves. He "comes only to kill, steal and destroy." Our battle is against him and his forces of evil, not against God and people.

About a year after the breakfast with my pastor, I was driving to a business lunch in downtown Denver in an area in which it was extremely difficult to find a parking space. I was concerned that I was going to be late for the meeting. The thought came into my mind to pray for a parking spot. Although God had been teaching me many lessons on how and when He answers prayer, I was afraid to pray for that. I didn't want to bother God with such a minor thing. The Holy Spirit persisted, "Pray for a parking spot." "What if He doesn't answer?" I thought to myself. It might shatter my belief in God and the progress I had made in my prayer life. "Pray for a parking spot," the Holy Spirit persisted again. So, I prayed for a parking spot. Within seconds, the traffic light turned red with five cars in front of me. Two men walked out of a store and got into a parked car. When the light changed to green, I waited until traffic pulled forward and let them out. Then I pulled into the parking spot and thanked God for teaching me that He does care about the small things in my life.

Praying in the Spirit is the most powerful piece of Armor to stop Satan from derailing you from becoming a mature Christian, receiving God's blessing and fulfilling The Great Commission – wherever you live or work.

PRAYING ON ALL OCCASIONS

Right on the heels of his description of the Armor of God, Paul adds that we should pray in the Spirit on all occasions *with all kinds of prayers and requests* (Ephesians 6:18).

As noted already, since we are equipped with God's armor, this implies that we are in His army. Since He is our Commander and knows the full battle plan to lead us to victory, it is easy to see the wisdom of maintaining a clear and constant line of communication with Him.

Since we don't always know how to pray as we should, if we have the Spirit in us and are led by that Spirit (Romans 8:14), Paul says the Spirit will make intercession for us. This means that although we do not always know exactly what we should be praying for, the Holy Spirit does.

In the same way, the Spirit helps us in our weakness. We do not know what we ought to pray for, but the Spirit Himself intercedes for us through wordless groans. And He who searches our hearts knows the mind of the Spirit, because the Spirit intercedes for God's people in accordance with the will of God (Romans 8:26-27).

Even when our requests are jumbled and confusing, God will always know what we are trying to say. He has intimate knowledge of our hearts and minds (after all, He created them). When we are unable to express ourselves or even discern what to pray for, the Spirit intercedes for us, in accordance with His will. He will always work things out for our best in the long run (Romans 8:28).

In what has become known as the 'Lord's Prayer,' Jesus Christ lays out for us a framework for praying to God. It is not a strict, inflexible format to be repeated by rote any time we come before God (Matthew 6:7), but rather an excellent framework of things we need to take the time to pray about daily. *In this manner, therefore, pray: Our Father in heaven, hallowed be Your name. Your kingdom come. Your will be done on earth as it is in heaven. Give us this day our daily bread. And forgive us our debts, as we forgive our debtors. And do not lead us into temptation, but deliver us from the evil one. For Yours is the kingdom and the power and the glory forever. Amen* (Matthew 6:9-13 NKJV).

Our God desires to provide us with the strength, wisdom and courage we need to stand against our enemies, but He will not force it on us. *Look to the Lord and His strength; seek His face always* (1 Chronicles 16:11). He wants us first to come before Him and ask for it. *The Lord will guide you always; He will satisfy your needs in a sun-scorched land and will strengthen your frame. You will be like a well-watered garden, like a spring whose waters never fail* (Isaiah 58:11).

The night before His crucifixion, Jesus was engaged in a spiritual war with Satan. He knew the outcome that His flesh desired. But He knew that His Father was always in charge and had everyone's eternal best interests in mind. When we are praying, it is important for us to pray for God's will to be done, too. *My Father, if it is possible, may this cup be taken from Me. Yet not as I will, but as You will* (Matthew 26:39).

Finally, we should be mindful to pray for fellow servants of God — not only ministers of the Gospel, but all God's people. We are in this battle together, and prayer is one of the most effective ways we can support each other, care for each other and fulfill the God-inspired command given to us in Philippians 2:4.13 [1]

SEVEN POWERFUL PRINCIPLES OF PRAYER

"We cannot stand if we do not pray because it is prayer that connects us, person to person, with our Great Savior" says Pastor Parker. Orthodox theology teaches that the Son of God is still both fully God and fully man, He is our great High Priest who understands what it is like to be us and to live our lives, facing the struggles we face. Right now, He is seated at the right hand of God the Father interceding for us (Hebrews 4:14-16). *Who is to condemn? Christ Jesus is the One who died—more than that, Who was raised—Who is at the right hand of God, Who indeed is interceding for us* (Romans 8:34).

American theologian Albert Barnes instructs us that, "No matter how complete the armor; no matter how skilled we may be in the science of war; no matter how courageous we may be, we may be certain that without prayer we shall be defeated. God alone can give the victory; and when the Christian soldier goes forth armed completely for the spiritual conflict, if he looks to God by prayer, he may be sure of a triumph."

The Bible teaches us powerful principles about prayer that can help us in life and our Spiritual War.

---

1 www.freebiblestudyguides.org

1. **Since Jesus experienced life as a human, you can approach Him with confidence** because He understands your difficulties in living life in this world. *For we do not have a high priest who is unable to empathize with our weaknesses, but we have One Who has been tempted in every way, just as we are—yet He did not sin* (Hebrews 4:15).
2. **Prayer is inseparable from your life** because the Holy Spirit, dwelling in us is also the One Who intercedes for us (Romans 8:26-27). *Because you are His sons, God sent the Spirit of His Son into our hearts, the Spirit Who calls out, "Abba, Father"* (Galatians 4:6). There is no separation between secular and spiritual. You have to put on the armor of God every day – all day. At work, with your family, socially and yes, even when you go to church. You do not live three lives – God, family and work. You live one life, and it is as a child of God the Father, a citizen of the Kingdom of God and a disciple of Jesus Christ, the King.
3. **The Holy Spirit helps us know how to pray** and He intercedes for us in our communications with the Father. *In the same way, the Spirit helps us in our weakness. We do not know what we ought to pray for, but the Spirit Himself intercedes for us through wordless groans. And He who searches our hearts knows the mind of the Spirit, because the Spirit intercedes for God's people in accordance with the will of God. And we know that in all things God works for the good of those who love Him, who have been called according to His purpose* (Romans 8:26-28).
4. **Jesus promises prayer power to those who have faith in Him.** The following Scripture has been one of the hardest ones for most Christians to grasp. I find it difficult, but practice believing it daily. If you, too, find it difficult (I don't know anyone who doesn't), I encourage all of us to ask God to increase our faith to receive and believe it, because Christ has proclaimed it to be the truth! *Very truly I tell you, **whoever** believes in Me will do*

the works I have been doing, and they will do even greater things than these, because I am going to the Father. And I will do whatever you ask in My name, so that the Father may be glorified in the Son. You may ask Me for anything in my name, and I will do it (John 14:12-14). **Maybe if we all just believed this, we would understand it and change the world.** Perhaps the basic problem in Christianity today is that people dismiss Scriptures that seem to them to be impossible and it greatly limits their spiritual growth and faith. As previously discussed, the first responsibility of leadership is to define reality. This is the Son of God, Leader of the Kingdom of God defining reality. Who among us are willing to dismiss the Word of the Son of God saying, "I tell you the truth?"

5. **"Prayer does not equip us for greater work – prayer is the greater work"** (Oswald Chambers). When our son, Barry (Bear), was about 24 we went to a Promise Keepers Christian conference in Colorado for men and their sons. Bear had been out of fellowship with the Lord for several years and didn't want to go with me. But one of our best friends from Minnesota was coming with his son Todd, who was a friend of Bear's. So he came with me – reluctant, frustrated and angry. His body language made it very clear that he didn't want to be there. At the opening night service he had sunglasses on. During the praise and worship time, he just looked straight ahead and didn't sing a note. The late Pastor E.V. Hill was the keynote speaker. His message was on "How to Make the Enemy Run." [2] **I started to pray for Bear, asking God to give him ears to hear with and eyes to see with.** I asked that God would give him understanding and insight into what he was hearing. Pastor Hill was teaching us how to use the Word of God to battle with Satan. The message was very insightful and powerful! All of a sudden, tears started to roll down Bear's face from

---

2 I highly recommend you go to the following web address to hear E.V. Hill's five minute video. His message is powerful! http://www.youtube.com/watch?v=5YDSgZ5c3iw.

under his sunglasses. The Holy Spirit was opening his eyes and softening his heart. Bear made a 180 degree turn in his spiritual life during that conference and he remembers it as the turning point in his life.

6. **Prayer can be used to protect and encourage the entire Body of Christ** while we are being sanctified, while we are coping with the world, and banding together in spiritual warfare, *And pray in the Spirit on all occasions with all kinds of prayers and requests. With this in mind, be alert and always keep on praying for all the Lord's people* (Ephesians 6:18).
7. **Pray in the Spirit.** To be in the Spirit, you must have your *minds set on what the Spirit desires* (Romans 8:5), not on what you desire. This includes a sincere decision to accept God's answer, enabling you to live in the "new nature" (Colossians 3:10 RSV), controlled by the Holy Spirit instead of living in your "old nature" (Ephesians 4:22), and as a result, enabling you to hold to Christ's teaching.

The Apostle Paul makes it clear who is in control and where the power lies when you pray, *I planted the seed, Apollos watered it, but God has been making it grow. So neither the one who plants nor the one who waters is anything, but only God, who makes things grow* (1 Corinthians 3:6-7).

EIGHT PRINCIPLES TO MAXIMIZE THE INFLUENCE OF PRAYER

The Bible also provides several helpful tips on how to maximize the influence of your prayers with God:

1. **Pray continuously and about everything, without anxiety.** Scripture instructs us to continually be in a state of prayer on all occasions and in all circumstances as you go through each day. Talk to God out loud or in your mind with thanksgiving, seeking his guidance and help

continuously as you live life, *Rejoice in the Lord always. I will say it again: Rejoice! Let your gentleness be evident to all. The Lord is near. Do not be anxious about anything, but in every situation, by prayer and petition, with thanksgiving, present your requests to God. And the peace of God, which transcends all understanding, will guard your hearts and your minds in Christ Jesus* (Philippians 4:4-7). I once prayed for grandchildren while driving to work one day. Ten months later our first grandchild was born – a beautiful granddaughter. And to make His point, God had her born on my birthday! Sometimes God answers prayer in a dramatic way to make it obvious to us that He is a personal God who is involved in our daily lives.

2. **Pray according to God's will, His instructions and promises in Scripture, then you will know it is His will.** What is God's will? There is no better way to find out than studying the Bible to understand what God's will is concerning your choices on earth. God cannot lie. Therefore, His teachings and promises are reality - the absolute truth about how to live life and make decisions that are pleasing to Him. God is faithful to His Covenant to fulfill The Promise to His children. Therefore, if you pray according to His will for you as revealed in Scripture, you will find your prayers to be much more powerful. By reading the Bible (learning truth) and applying it, you will know God's will and ways (Romans 12: 1-2). In studying the Bible back in the mid 1990's, I discovered that it is not God's desire for us to be in debt. In fact, Deuteronomy 28 teaches us that if we obey God's commands we will be a lender and not a borrower. So Ree Ann and I prayed that

God would show us how to get out of debt. Today we have no debt, including our home. How did He do it? Looking back, I'm not entirely sure! But how God worked in our lives may or may not be how He wants to work in your life. If you want to get out of debt, ask Him to help you, obey what He tells you to do, and He will show you the way.

3. **Be persistent and patient.** *Ask and it will be given to you; seek and you will find; knock and the door will be opened to you. For everyone who asks receives; the one who seeks finds; and to the one who knocks, the door will be opened... If you, then, though you are evil, know how to give good gifts to your children, how much more will your Father in heaven give good gifts to those who ask Him* (Matthew 7:7-11)! In the Greek, the words, "ask," "seek," and "knock" are in the "present imperative active" voice, meaning "keep on asking," "keep on seeking" and "keep on knocking." My wife made me a framed cross-stitch of these verses in 1989, and it has been hanging in my offices at work ever since. It has always been a great visual reminder and encouragement for me to keep on seeking truth in Scripture and trusting God in my suffering, trials and successes.

4. **Develop an attitude of trusting God's judgment/ wisdom.** Accept the fact that God has absolute sovereignty over your life. As children of God, we are encouraged in the Bible to always remember who we are and conduct ourselves accordingly. We are also instructed to remember who we are not. There is only One God and He has absolute sovereignty over us. He rules with love, justice, mercy, grace and ways that we don't always understand. Sometimes his answer to our prayers is "No" - or "Temporarily, no" - as

He teaches or tests us. I have found that sometimes it may take Him years to answer prayers. We do not always have the big picture, but He always does!

5. **Check your motives when asking for His help,** *You do not have, because you do not ask God. When you ask, you do not receive, because you ask with wrong motives, that you may spend what you get on your pleasures* (James 4:2-3).
6. **Check your relationship with your wife,** *Husbands, in the same way be considerate as you live with your wives, and treat them with respect as the weaker partner and as heirs with you of the gracious gift of life, so that nothing will hinder your prayers* (1 Peter 3:7).
7. **Have a simple faith in Him as a child to a father,** *Which of you fathers, if your son asks for a fish, will give him a snake instead? Or if he asks for an egg, will give him a scorpion? If you then, though you are evil, know how to give good gifts to your children, how much more will your Father in heaven give the Holy Spirit (the Spirit of truth and wisdom) to those who ask Him* (Luke 11:11-13). Ree Ann is much better at this than I am.
8. **Make sure your behavior and choices** demonstrate an earnest belief in the existence of God. *And without faith it is impossible to please God, because anyone who comes to Him must believe that He exists and that He rewards those who earnestly seek Him* (Hebrews 11:6).

In 1973, I had a conversation with the late Dr. Vernon Grounds. We were discussing why God would move me one thousand miles to a job that was obviously only going to last four months. His reply was "God is the great chess player." Looking back on my life now, I better understand what God was doing at the time. Since His ways are not our ways, it is better to trust His judgment about everything He teaches us! By this I mean don't defy His teaching, judgment and wisdom. Just trust and obey Him. This does not mean we can't ask Him "why" questions. In Jeremiah 33:3, He says *Call to Me and I will answer you and tell you great and unsearchable things you do not know.*

The Apostle Paul reminds us that God is, ultimately, in control: *What then shall we say? Is God unjust? Not at all! For He says to Moses, 'I will have mercy on whom I have mercy, and I will have compassion on whom I have compassion.' It does not, therefore, depend on human desire or effort, but on God's mercy. For Scripture says to Pharaoh: 'I raised you up for this very purpose, that I might display My power in you and that My name might be proclaimed in all the earth.' Therefore God has mercy on whom He wants to have mercy, and He hardens whom He wants to harden. One of you will say to me: 'Then why does God still blame us? For who is able to resist His will?' But who are you, a human being, to talk back to God? 'Shall what is formed say to the One Who formed it, 'Why did you make me like this?' Does not the potter have the right to make out of the same lump of clay some pottery for special purposes and some for common use* (Romans 9:14-21)?

Each person has been given the freedom to choose whether he/she will uphold his/her obligation under the Covenant Promise. Your choices affect your relationship with God, the use of His supernatural power in your life, your protection and your rewards on earth as well as in the next life. **Choose wisely!**

REMEMBER K.I.S.S.? KEEP IT SIMPLE, SAINT

Jesus tells us that *The work of God is this: to believe in the One He has sent* (John 6:29). That's it! That is our responsibility under The

Covenant. Christ is the way, the truth and the life.

All creation was made through Jesus Christ and He is King and Lord over all of Creation! All living beings, including demons, fear Him because of His power (James 2:19)! He is your King, as well as your Savior (See John 18:37)! He understands you and cares about you (Hebrews 2:14)! He is your High Priest (Hebrews 4:14)! He is the Mediator between you and God the Father (1 Timothy 2:5)!

All authority in Heaven and on Earth has been given to Him and He is with you always (Matthew 28:18-20)! Apart from Jesus, you can do nothing (John 15:5). **Nothing!!!**

About twenty years ago I began praying every day that God would give me wisdom, knowledge and understanding in Kingdom, personal, family and business matters. God gave me the following verses as my life verses: *My goal is that they may be encouraged in heart and united in love, so that they may have the full riches of complete understanding, in order that they may know the mystery of God, namely, Christ, in Whom are hidden all the treasures of wisdom and knowledge. I tell you this so that no one may deceive you by fine-sounding arguments* (Colossians 2:2-4). If you seek Him with all your heart, you too can learn to apply these spiritual principles and concepts in the marketplace, right where you are – whether you are a street sweeper or a Fortune 500 CEO!

You are praying to and building a relationship with a Person of power far beyond your imagination! He literally holds the power of life and death, blessings and curses. I have asked Christ about many things concerning life on this earth, fallen prey to some of Satan's schemes and made many mistakes in my spiritual growth walk. But my earthly father taught me to "keep your eyes on Jesus." Therefore, I have learned to respect Jesus Christ's position as King and I go to

Him daily for grace and mercy, direction and insights on *the way, the truth and the life* (John 14: 6).

I still have a lot to learn, so I "keep my eyes on Jesus" every day.

"NOT BY MIGHT NOR BY POWER,
BUT **BY MY SPIRIT,"**
SAYS THE LORD ALMIGHTY.

The Prophet Zechariah

If you remain in Me and My words remain in you, ask whatever you wish, and it will be done for you.

John 15:7

QUESTIONS FOR CONSIDERATION:

- What does it mean to pray in the Spirit?
- What are seven powerful principles concerning prayer? How can you use them in your career or business?
- What are eight ways to maximize the influence of your prayers with God?
- How are you going to apply the K.I.S.S principle in your life and career/business?
- Name three specific ways you are going to increase the effectiveness of your prayers.

The devil said to Him,
"If you are the Son of God,
tell this stone
to become bread."
Jesus answered
"It is written..."
Luke 4:3-4
STAND
FIRM
WITH THE FULL ARMOR

CHAPTER 11

STAND FIRM

The Apostle John instructs believers in Christ that, *whoever claims to live in Him must live as Jesus did* (1 John 2:6). Once you spend the time to really know and understand who you are in Christ and how to properly put on and use the full armor of God, you can "live as Jesus did." He didn't use His Own supernatural power, but relied on the supernatural power of His Father living in Him, *Who, though He was in the form of God, did not regard equality with God as something to be exploited, but emptied Himself, taking the form of a slave, being born in human likeness* (Philippians 2:6-7 NRSV).

Since the children have flesh and blood, He too shared in their humanity so that by His death He might break the power of him who holds the power of death—that is, the devil—and free those who all their lives were held in slavery by their fear of death. For surely it is not angels He helps, but Abraham's descendants. For this reason He had to be made like them, fully human in every way, in order that He might become a merciful and faithful high priest in service to God, and that He might make atonement for the sins of the people. Because He Himself suffered when He was tempted, He is able to help those who are being tempted (Hebrews 2:14-18).

How did Jesus live and stand firm while He was on earth? He explains how He did it:

» *It is the Father, living in Me, who is doing His work* (John 14:10).

» *The One who sent Me is with Me; He has not left Me alone, for I always do what pleases Him"* (John 8:29).

» *I love the Father and do exactly what My Father has commanded Me"* (John 14:31).

» *Jesus answered, "It is written..." When the devil had finished all this tempting, he left him until an opportune time* (Luke 4:4 & 13).

Relying on His Father's power and not His own, *Jesus went through all the towns and villages... proclaiming the good news of the kingdom* (Matthew 9:35). That is how you are to live, when you trust and obey Him, His supernatural power is "with you" and He renders the old nature "dead" – powerless.

Apostle Paul instructs us in Ephesians 6, that *"after you have done everything...stand firm,"* What does Paul mean *"after you have done everything"*? He is referring back to what he wrote in the book of Ephesians. You will stay fully connected to the Vine if you obey Christ (John 14 and 15). If you don't obey Him, you are like a branch half broken, limp and barely alive with some nourishment reaching its starving ends, but powerless to thrive and grow.

But when you follow His commands and teaching, He is with you. Therefore, you are fully connected to the Vine (John 15), growing, thriving and producing fruit. When He is with you, it is not you doing these things; it is God the Father and the Lord Jesus

Christ living in you who is doing them. You will receive an anointing of the Holy Spirit that will empower you to go through life "doing good" and "proclaiming the good news of the Kingdom." That is how Jesus did it while on earth; *It is the Father, living in Me, who is doing His work. The One who sent Me is with Me; He has not left Me alone, for I always do what pleases Him* (John 8:29). *I love the Father and do exactly what My Father has commanded Me* (John 14:31).

Note that Paul begins his message about the armor of God in Ephesians 6 with the word, "Finally." This indicates that it would be a wise idea to read the whole book of Ephesians, to see how Paul encourages us to prepare to defeat Satan and the forces of darkness. Then, we will be better able to stand our ground against Satan and win the struggles against the flesh, the world, and Satan in the marketplace.

What does Paul mean when he tells us to stand firm? When faced with danger, we humans experience what is called the "fight or flight" response.

THE FIGHT OR FLIGHT RESPONSE

Dr. Neil F. Neimark MD, from the Mind/Body Education Center offers us some great insight about what the "fight or flight" response is and how it affects our judgment:

"The 'fight or flight response' is our body's… automatic, inborn response that prepares the body to 'fight' or 'flee' from perceived attack, harm or threat to our survival. When we experience excessive stress—whether from internal worry or external circumstance—a bodily reaction is triggered, called the 'fight or flight' response. This response is hard-wired into our brains and represents a genetic wisdom designed to protect us from bodily harm. This response actually corresponds to an area of our brain called the hypothalamus, which—when stimulated—initiates a sequence of nerve cell firing and chemical release that prepares our body for running or fighting. What are the signs that our fight or flight response has been activated? When our fight or flight response is activated, sequences of nerve cell firing occur and chemicals like adrenaline, noradrenaline and cortisol are released into our bloodstream. These patterns of nerve cell firing and chemical release cause our body to undergo a series of very dramatic changes. Our respiratory rate increases. Blood is shunted away from our digestive tract and directed into our muscles and limbs, which require extra energy and fuel for running and fighting. Our pupils dilate. Our awareness intensifies. Our sight sharpens. Our impulses quicken. Our perception of pain diminishes. Our immune system mobilizes with increased activation. We become prepared—physically and psychologically—for fight or flight. We scan and search our environment, looking for the enemy.

"When our fight or flight system is activated, we tend to perceive everything in our environment as a possible threat to our survival. By its very nature, the fight or flight system bypasses our rational mind—where our more well thought out beliefs exist—and moves us into "attack" mode. This state of alert causes us to perceive almost everyone and everything in our world as a possible enemy. Like airport security during a terrorist threat, we are on the lookout for every possible danger. We may overreact to the slightest comment. Our fear is exaggerated. Our thinking is distorted. We see everything through the filter of possible danger. We narrow our focus to those things that can harm us. Fear becomes the lens through which we see the world.

"It is almost impossible to cultivate positive attitudes and beliefs when we are stuck in survival mode. Our heart is not open. Our rational mind is disengaged. Our consciousness is focused on fear, not love. Making clear choices and recognizing the consequences of those choices is not feasible. We are focused on short-term survival, not the long-term consequences of our beliefs and choices. When we are overwhelmed with excessive stress, our life becomes a series of short-term emergencies. We lose the ability to relax and enjoy the moment. We live from crisis to crisis, with no relief in sight. Burnout is inevitable. This burnout is what usually provides the motivation to change our lives for the better. We are propelled to step back and look at the big picture of our lives—forcing us to examine our beliefs, our values and our goals."

THE OPTION TO FIGHT OR FLIGHT

Satan often uses this fight or flight response to persuade us to see people as the threat, instead of him. Amazingly, he can even twist the meaning of Scripture around in a person's mind, so that they see God as the threat, instead of him. He can persuade people to see the world as the threat, instead of him. And he can also get us to see our sinful nature as the threat, instead of him. By doing so, we fight with everybody we encounter: family, friends, co-workers, strangers and even ourselves. Or, we take flight, escaping from perceived danger, avoiding pain and suffering, escaping reality, and eluding responsibilities. By doing so, we are missing the fullness of life and purpose and blessings God has planned for us.

The Apostle Paul speaks of another alternative to the fight or flight response, *Epaphras, who is one of you and a servant of Christ Jesus, sends greetings. He is always wrestling in prayer for you,* ***that you may stand firm in all the will of God, mature and fully assured*** (Colossians 4:12). Paul here presents us with the better choice - to stand! When you stand, you are not running or fighting, you are trusting God to be "with you," supernaturally helping you with all aspects of your life and with Satan's schemes. As you mature in Christ, you become fully assured of truth (reality) and His will for you. You learn the reality: 1) that your battle is not against people - flesh and blood - but against Satan and his forces of evil, 2) that you do not have the power to win the battle against Satan and his forces of evil, and 3) that God and only God can defeat Satan and the forces of evil because He is more powerful than them and therefore, they fear Him!

You, on the other hand, "stand firm" on God's promises and truth - He cannot lie! You stand firm and let Christ the King and His angels fight for you! When you have problems with people, you go to God in prayer, ask Him for help, ask how you should pray about the matter and ask Him what you need to do to improve the situation.

When the forces of darkness come at you with one of their schemes, you stand and say to Satan, "It is written" and then quote an appropriate Scripture that you have memorized or ask the Holy Spirit to give you one in the moment! Then command the devil in the name of Jesus Christ to leave you! *What, then, shall we say in response to this? If God is for us, who can be against us? No, in all these things we are more than conquerors through Him who loved us. For I am convinced that neither death nor life, neither angels nor demons, neither the present nor the future, nor any powers, neither height nor depth, nor anything else in all creation, will be able to separate us from the love of God that is in Christ Jesus our Lord* (Romans 8:31,37-39).

If your faith is weak, ask God to increase it as the father of the demoniac did: *"I do believe; help me overcome my unbelief"* (Mark 9:24)! *I tell you the truth, if you have faith as small as a mustard seed, you can say to this mountain, "Move from here to there" and it will move. Nothing will be impossible for you* (Matthew 17:20).

THE LORD WAS WITH HIM

"Most believers live by the measure of God's grace that they appropriate in their lives. But very few people prepare themselves and work for the favor of God that they can easily avail. When God's favor is poured out on someone, it makes a world of difference in his or her life" (From Bethel Articles).

The LORD ***was with*** *Joseph, so he succeeded in everything he did as he served in the home of his Egyptian master* (Genesis 39:2 NLT). The phrase, "God was with…" or "the Lord was with…" someone has a very significant meaning in Scripture. It represents a close fellowship and trust between God and that person.

When God is with you, you are living under His supernatural hedge of protection and shower of blessings. "No plottings of men, no combinations of circumstances can defeat the man who has God as his helper. Here is the secret of many a life, conspired against by ill health, poverty, evil men, foes in the household, the world, the flesh and the devil, but victorious, anyway – God was with him. The devil and men often overstep themselves; sell Joseph into Egypt, but God makes him Prime Minister" (Dr. Vance Havner)!

Remember in the introduction, we saw a long list of people in the Bible who God *was with* and they enjoyed favor with Him? They were just normal people like you and me. But every one of them had one thing in common. They believed that God exists and that He rewards those who earnestly seek Him (Hebrews 11:6). They demonstrated their faith by following His teachings and obeying His commands. Their stories illustrate to us that they didn't do this perfectly. But when they failed, they repented and stayed the course.

KEEPING GOD WITH YOU

There can be times, perhaps many times in a Christian's life when God seems to be very far away from us. It may even feel as though He has left us altogether. God is not one for breaking promises. Faith can become so obscured by what we are feeling that we find it impossible to see where God is in our situation or journey. Whenever we find ourselves thinking this way, we must test all such thoughts against Scripture. These are lies from Satan to make us think that we have been forsaken. As a child of God, that will never happen. We must not let feelings overcome us, determine our beliefs or order our steps.

Nevertheless, as you work in the business domain, be very discerning about your choices - and the thoughts in your mind that you base them on. Your choices do affect your fellowship and relationship with your Heavenly Father and the Lord Jesus Christ. Be careful about assessing God's blessing on your life by how much money you make or don't make or how smoothly things are going in your business life. Satan is every bit as capable of "blessing" you with money and power as God is. Consider how he tempted Christ. *Again, the devil took Him to a very high mountain and showed Him all the kingdoms of the world and their splendor. 'All this I will give you,' He said, 'if you will bow down and worship me'* (Matthew 4:8).

How does one worship and/or serve Satan, you ask? You worship him by holding to his teaching, operating his way and following his leading in your life instead of those of God the Father and the Lord Jesus Christ. "I don't do that," you say. Are you sure?

Do you know that you *know* God's teaching, ways and leading in your mind? God's ways and Satan's ways are twisted together in the cultures on this earth. It can be easy to confuse them in our minds, especially if we are under a lot of stress and pressure to perform.

What is the solution? Choose to always do it God's way so that He is continuously with you. That is, His supernatural blessings and protection are on your life. He is blessing your work and has a hedge of protection around you like He did Job. Read the word of God and ask the Holy Spirit to lead you to the truth, developing your personal spiritual discernment. Enjoy God's calling to work in the business domain. Help Christ build His Church right where you are. When you mess up, ask God to forgive you and move on.

For most of my Christian life I got the impression that The Great Commission was just about evangelism, going out into the world sharing Christ with others. Whenever the topic came up, the discussions were always about sharing Christ with someone resulting in them accepting Him into their life as Lord and Savior. A very good thing indeed! Everyone would celebrate and then go about their lives. But one day in 2010, I was preparing for a meeting with business owners to discuss Michael Baer's book *Business as Mission*, when the following words (in bold) from Matthew 28:18-20 jumped off the page like silver bullets from a gun: *Then Jesus came to them and said, 'All authority in heaven and on earth has been given to Me. Therefore* ***go and make disciples*** *of all nations, baptizing them in the name of the Father and of the Son and of the Holy Spirit, and* ***teaching them to obey everything I have commanded you.*** *And surely I am with you always, to the very end of the age.*

The Holy Spirit led me to look deeper into what Christ really commanded Christians to do - showing me that Christ commissioned all Christians to make disciples, not just converts. Christ mentored and trained His recruits concerning truth about God and His Kingdom, the spiritual war with Satan and his forces of darkness and to help usher in the Kingdom of God on earth. Jesus taught them how to distinguish a true disciple. *To the Jews who had believed Him, Jesus said, 'If you hold to My teaching, you are really My disciples'* (John 8:31).

There is no uncertainty in what Christ is saying here. If a person is really His disciple, he or she will hold to His teaching. This means His disciples will be intentional about following His teaching, they will obey Him and they will train others to obey everything He has commanded.

I began doing my own personal survey. For about a year I asked many marketplace Christians and Christian leaders in the religious domain what their perception of The Great Commission was. Only one could quote it and almost all of them gave me an answer that described only evangelism – sharing Christ with people and baptizing them. Like me, they were surprised to learn or recall that Jesus told us to: *make disciples, teaching them to obey* His commands.

Last week, while writing this book, I met with a Christian attorney, a good man. We were discussing this topic. "Is that my job?" he asked and continued with, "That's the job of the churches." We continued to discuss Christ's Mission. He continued, "I barely have time to fulfill all my obligations to clients and family." While he was talking, I felt his pain and understood exactly what he was saying. Looking back at the times I was building businesses having the same feelings and thoughts, like this attorney, I lacked understanding of the power of God being with me. He cares about us having a balanced life and as such, He helps us with His power and understanding to obtain that balance.

Every Christian is called to be a disciple of Christ in some way. What that way is for you is between you and God. And, although many Christians don't believe discipling others can be done in the business domain because of legal issues, people in the business domain around the world are finding ways to do it. And with the full Armor on, you can Stand Firm.

FINALLY, BE STRONG IN THE LORD AND IN HIS MIGHTY POWER

The Apostle Paul concludes his instructions to the saints in Ephesus as follows: ***Finally, be strong in the Lord and in His mighty power. Put on the full armor of God,*** *so that you can take your stand against the devil's schemes. For our struggle is not against flesh and blood, but against the rulers, against the authorities, against the powers of this dark world and against the spiritual forces of evil in the heavenly realms. Therefore put on the full armor of God, so that when the day of evil comes, you may be able to stand your ground,* ***and after you have done everything, to stand. Stand firm…*** (Ephesians 6:10-14).

Do not battle with people. Do not battle with your flesh. Just quote Scripture to Satan, believe the Scripture and then trust in God's power. *I will deliver this vast army into your hands, and you will know that I am the LORD* (1 Kings 20:28). When the devil attacks you – "Hit him!" If you haven't done it yet, I highly recommend that you listen to the late Pastor E.V. Hill's video at this time. Even if you already listened to it, you may want to listen to it again.

Now turn it over to Him who is able to do immeasurably more than all we ask or imagine, according to His power that is at work within us, to Him be glory in the church and in Christ Jesus throughout all generations, for ever and ever! Amen (Ephesians 3:20-21).

NOW IT IS GOD
WHO MAKES BOTH US AND YOU
STAND FIRM IN CHRIST.
HE ANOINTED US,
SET HIS SEAL OF OWNERSHIP ON US,
AND PUT HIS SPIRIT IN OUR HEARTS
AS A DEPOSIT,
GUARANTEEING WHAT IS TO COME.

The Apostle Paul

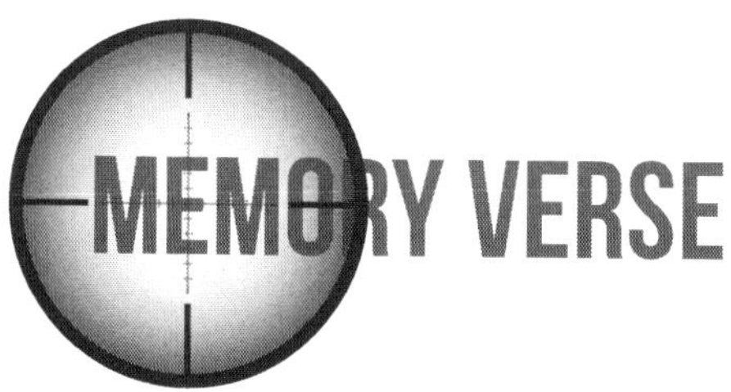

It is written.

Luke 4:4

QUESTIONS FOR CONSIDERATION:

- What is the "fight or flight" response? How does it relate to your life, career or business?
- What does Paul mean to "stand firm"? How can you apply it to your life, career or business?
- How do you prepare to be able to "stand"? What do Christ and Paul teach about this?
- Why is it important to have on the full Armor of God? When should you have it on?
- What is your action plan to prepare for battle with Satan and the forces of evil?
- What are your most important takeaways concerning the Armor of God?

Then Jesus
came to them and said,
"All authority in heaven and on earth
has been given to me.
Therefore **go and make disciples**
of all nations, baptizing them
in the name of the Father
and of the Son
and of the Holy Spirit,
and **teaching them**
to obey everything
I have commanded you.
And surely I am with you always,
to the very end of the age."

Mathew 28:18-20

CALL TO HONOR

CHAPTER 12

CALL TO HONOR

The principles and concepts of truth outlined in this book are transferable and applicable to every domain of your life including business, home, personal, spiritual, social, etc. They are applicable in your finances, marriage, family, friendships and all relationships with both God and people. Take them with you to apply in every part of your life! God will be with you as you do.

As a teenager attending the Billy Sunday Memorial Tabernacle in Sioux City, Iowa, we used to sing *Onward Christian Solders* on a regular basis. Of course, at that age, I just thought it was a cool song. I had no idea what I was really singing about. I thought it was just about winning souls, having fun working together, sharing Jesus Christ with others so they could have eternal life, too. But I was unaware I was in a real war or how that subtle war in my mind or that of my family and friends could and would impact the outcomes of our lives.

Satan is very crafty about the way he integrates his ideas into your mind and judgment as you work and make decisions in life. Look at the job he did on Eve! My entire career has been in the business domain as an entrepreneur, CPA and business advisor working with hundreds of companies and numerous business professionals. During these years I have been in thousands of meetings brainstorming decisions, both small and significant. One thing I have learned with certainty, the human mind is capable of rationalizing anything! Let's take for example "the end justifies the means" rationalization. I have seen this used many times in the business and non-profit domain. The following story discusses an example that integrates both the business and the religious domains.

A LEGEND DESTROYED

In 1973 my wife and I moved our family to Colorado to accept a position of Controller and Chief Financial Officer of a prominent non-profit conglomerate which comprised a large church, a large nursing home, a trust and a foundation (four different entities I will call "The Ministries"). The nursing home was in financial trouble and the church was raising money by selling what they called "CDs" (they were really notes and bonds). The pastor of the church was a highly respected man who was known around the world. He had enjoyed a highly successful career and could do no wrong in the eyes of his peers, his board, his Executive VP, his management team and his congregation.

The Board of Trustees of the church hired me to find out why the nursing home was losing so much money and what had caused the crisis. They had never seen a financial statement of the nursing home. One of the reasons they hired me was because I was instrumental in helping to rewrite the cost reimbursement law for nursing homes in Minnesota.

I arrived at work the first day to find a cash report on my desk prepared by the controller of the nursing home reflecting that it was about $250,000 overdrawn at the bank. The Executive VP (EVP) of The Ministries had left on vacation, so I went to the controller and asked him if the EVP had a plan for covering the overdraft. "No", he replied "he just said he would pray about it." That was the best day of my employment at The Ministries.

After some analysis and evaluation, I found that the nursing home was on an impossible financial mission. The pricing, cost and margin structure would not carry the debt load of the company, part of which was because they had paid too much for the nursing home. As a result of that debt and loans to finance property improvements, interest and operating losses, they were compounding their debt annually by millions of dollars. They were covering those cash shortages by selling more and more church CDs to the public to keep The Ministries going and protect the reputation of their pastor.

They were selling the church CDs and loaning the money to the nursing home because the SEC had given them an order to stop selling nursing home CDs. Money had been and was being moved from entity to entity like pawns on a chess board. Lies were being told to the public and the church board and information withheld to keep them from knowing what was going on. At one of the board meetings I asked if their SEC attorney had approved the selling of CDs by the church and loaning the money to the nursing home. The pastor quickly said yes, he had checked that out. The next day I called the attorney (who, although I was the CFO, I was told by the EVP not to have any contact with) and asked him if he was aware of the practice. He got very angry and said he had specifically told the pastor to stop doing that.

I continued to do significant investigation of the people who had been running the nursing home and financial information and could go on with many more stories about this experience. At age 29, the most puzzling thing to me about the whole experience was that almost no one would listen to the facts. For the first time in my life, I experienced the "halls of power," a fierce loyalty to a person who could do no wrong in their eyes. After about 90 days, I put together consolidated financial statements and supporting information of The Ministries. It showed that they had about $20 million in assets at market value and $27 million in debt. They were losing money at a rate of about $1.5 million per year and they needed about $1 million to cover their obligations for the next 90 days. The Ministries were incapable of raising that much money so quickly without raising a lot of questions and concerns. I recommended that they file a voluntary reorganization bankruptcy. I also recommended that they actually turn over control of the finances to me as the CFO. They declined to do either of those and I was told the next day my services would no longer be needed. Four months later they were forced into bankruptcy. Eventually the pastor was charged and convicted of fraud.

The sad part of this story is that it appeared to me that – for most of this pastor's career - he was a good and honest man. God had been "with him" and he had a very powerful and effective ministry. But at a vulnerable time, he obviously started listening to the wrong voices, using the "end justifies the means" rationalization. He began to lie and use deception – strategies of Satan, not of the Kingdom of God. I am sure all that was rational in his mind because of all the good The Ministries were doing. But, he was violating key principles of The Kingdom of God. Eventually, when he would not listen to the sound counsel of very competent people around him, repent and change his ways, God removed His anointing from him and was no longer "with him." Everything stopped working.

There are other key mistakes in sound judgment involved in this story that were caused by not properly defining reality and the misapplication of faith in God. They violated sound Biblical financial principles to the point where they were testing God. And like Satan tempting Jesus to throw Himself off the highest point of the temple and call upon the Father to rescue Him, they were just being foolish. The pastor and other key leaders should have followed Jesus' teachings – and His response to Satan and answered *"It says, 'Do not put the Lord your God to the test'"* (Luke 4:12). Then, God's full protection and blessings would have stayed with them.

WHY THE GREAT COMMISSION?

The answer to this question may surprise you! You may be thinking, "So people can go to heaven when they die," or "To save people from hell." These are true and significant, but they do not explain God's big picture. He has much bigger objectives in mind! His objectives are to save and restore mankind back to their original nature made in the image of God, have "a people" to fellowship with, build His Church, restore creation, and re-establish rule of His Kingdom reign on earth! Let's look at these objectives one at a time:

To save and restore mankind back to their original nature made in the image of God. In the beginning, all that was necessary for God to create was His words. He simply said, Light, be! and light was. But when He created man, there was a Triune decision to determine the nature of man (Genesis 1:26). This indicates the unique dignity, moral excellence and God-like nature of this created being. When God breathed into his nostrils, man became the only part of creation to receive the breath of life (Genesis 2:7). According to some Hebrew scholars, this is the point at which man became a rational soul. Since God cannot die, the life imparted to Adam was eternal. Man received the immortal nature of God! [1]

In other words, man was created "a chip off the old block." We were created in the sinless image and immortal likeness of God. Then, after Adam and Eve's disobedience, our God nature was distorted by sin (a deadly condition) entering our human bodies. That is why Christ came, so that through faith in Him, those who believe can be restored back to God's image:

» *Do not lie to one another, seeing that you have put off the old nature with its practices and have put on the new nature, which is being renewed in knowledge after the image of its Creator* (Colossians 3:9-10 RSV).

» *Put off your old nature which belongs to your former manner of life and is corrupt through deceitful lusts, and be renewed in the spirit of your minds, and put on the new nature, created after the likeness of God in true righteousness and holiness* (Ephesians 4:22-24 RSV).

To continue what God started at the creation of man, making for Himself a people He could have fellowship with – the family of God.

» *But to all who received Him, who believed in His name, He gave power to become children of God; who were born, not of blood nor of the will of the flesh nor of the will of man, but of God* (John 1:12-13).

» *Both the one who makes people holy and those who are made holy are of the same family. So Jesus is not ashamed to call them brothers and sisters* (Hebrews 2:11).

» *My dwelling place will be with them; I will be their God, and they will be My people* (Ezekiel 37:27).

To restore all of creation to its perfect and pure Edenic state.

---

1 Paraphrased from A. Jones, The Biblical Illustrator

» *For all creation is waiting eagerly for that future day when God will reveal who His children really are. Against its will, all creation was subjected to God's curse. But with eager hope, the creation looks forward to the day when it will join God's children in glorious freedom from death and decay. For we know that all creation has been groaning as in the pains of childbirth right up to the present time. And we believers also groan, even though we have the Holy Spirit within us as a foretaste of future glory, for we long for our bodies to be released from sin and suffering. We, too, wait with eager hope for the day when God will give us our full rights as His adopted children, including the new bodies He has promised us* (Romans 8:19-23 NLT).

To build up the Church, the presence of the Kingdom of God on earth.

» *I will build My church, and the gates of Hades will not overcome it* (Matthew 16:18).

Christ made it clear that there would be resistance from the forces of evil! He also makes it clear that He would assist us in standing against them. But what is the conflict all about? The answer seems to have been lost, or at least, watered down in the religion of Christianity, versus the reality of Christianity.

What does the word "church" mean? In the Greek the word used is *ekklesia*, which means "assembly." It is derived from ek, meaning 'out of,' and klesis, meaning 'a calling.' This word was used among the Greeks of a body of citizens 'gathered' to discuss the affairs of state. To Christians, it has two applications: (a) the whole company of the redeemed throughout the present era, the company of which Christ said, 'I will build My Church,' and (b) a company consisting of professed believers. [2]

2 Source: Vine's Expository Dictionary of Biblical Words

The Apostle Peter tells the believers in Christ they are a royal priesthood, a holy nation, God's special possession. That nation is the Kingdom of God, a holy nation with a government of which Christ is the King. As such, you are citizens of God's Kingdom and joint heirs with Christ, a royal priesthood.

In the first century church, Christians assembled together not only to worship God but also to discuss the affairs of state. You may be thinking they were there to discuss how to build the Church and increase the Kingdom of God on earth. How is that "affairs of state?"

The objective revealed in the book of Revelation is for Christ and the citizens of the Kingdom to rule on earth! As the Body of Christ grows, the Kingdom becomes a greater threat to Satan, who is the current ruler of this world. Therefore, the battle intensifies - as we are witnessing in the world today! If you want to know what is going on in a nation, organization, company or family, look into the vision, mind and behavior of the leader. God shows us His ultimate vision for our world in Revelation 11:15:

» *The seventh angel sounded his trumpet, and there were loud voices in heaven, which said: 'The kingdom of the world has become the kingdom of our Lord and of His Messiah, and He will reign for ever and ever.'*

» And the enemy doesn't like it. *He* (Satan) *is filled with fury, because he knows that his time is short* (Revelations 12:12b).

At the end of the story, Satan and his forces are thrown into the pit and Christ takes over rule of Planet Earth with the believers in Christ ruling with Him.

» *And I saw an angel coming down out of heaven, having the key to the Abyss and holding in his hand a great chain. He seized the dragon, that ancient serpent, who is the devil, or Satan, and bound him for a thousand years. He threw him*

> *into the Abyss, and locked and sealed it over him, to keep him from deceiving the nations anymore until the thousand years were ended. After that, he must be set free for a short time (Revelation 20:1-3). When the thousand years are over, Satan will be released from his prison and will go out to deceive the nations in the four corners of the earth — Gog and Magog — and to gather them for battle. In number they are like the sand on the seashore. They marched across the breadth of the earth and surrounded the camp of God's people, the city He loves. But fire came down from heaven and devoured them. And the devil, who deceived them, was thrown into the lake of burning sulfur, where the beast and the false prophet had been thrown. They will be tormented day and night for ever and ever* (Revelation 20:1-10).

There you have the big picture! In the present time we have two kingdoms in conflict over the future rule of Planet Earth - a cosmic battle between God & Satan, with you in the middle! Satan, currently the ruler over this world, at war with King Jesus, represented on earth by the Body of Christ. That is, the children of God whose mission on Earth is building the Kingdom of God one disciple at a time - freeing those who will obey His teaching from the grip of the lethal condition in man: sin - living in them. Their purpose includes rescuing the believers in Jesus Christ from the bondage of Satan and his schemes being implemented by his forces of darkness. Satan's goal is to stop the advance of Christ's Church.

For this reason, since the day we heard about you, we have not stopped praying for you and asking God to fill you with the knowledge of His will through all the wisdom and understanding that the Spirit gives, so that you may live a life worthy of the Lord and please Him in every way: bearing fruit in every good work, growing in the knowledge of God, being strengthened with all power according to His glorious might so that you may have great endurance and patience, and giving joyful thanks to the Father, who has qualified you to share in the inheritance of

His holy people in the kingdom of light. For He has rescued us from the dominion of darkness and brought us into the kingdom of the Son He loves (Colossians 1:9-13).

THE CALL TO HONOR

Who needs *The Lord of the Rings* to experience a great adventure? Every Christian is called by the Lord of the universe to a great adventure! If you call yourself a Christian, you are claiming His name and therefore His Mission. The Bible says the Body of Christ is responsible to usher in the Kingdom of God on earth. There is no back-up plan! God has made each of us unique with a special purpose (John 15:16).

For Christians, there is no separation between secular and spiritual life! God, family, work and personal is not four different lives. Christians live one life and it is all for Him who called them according to His purpose. So, if you are wondering what His purpose for your life is, you can be assured that it is included, in some fashion, in His master plan outlined in this chapter.

The forces of darkness are advancing all around the world with fear, lies and deception, sidetracking and sidelining members of the Body of Christ. Together with their leader, Satan, these evil forces work in the minds and hearts of billions of people, masquerading as angels of light and deceiving them into believing that right is wrong and wrong is right (2 Corinthians 11:14-15). They work in Christian denominations to create confusion and disunity. They make you afraid to help build the Kingdom of God on earth and assist you in rationalizing that it is not your job and that you don't have time.

Being a disciple of Christ is not what you do, it is who you are! You are ambassadors of the King of the Kingdom of God, a holy nation, present on earth as the Body of Christ. For most of us in the marketplace, His high calling is for us to be salt and light right where we are, using the talents and gifts He created us with, in the business domain - as owners, leaders, managers, professionals or employees – making disciples as Christ leads us.

» *You are the salt of the earth. But if the salt loses its saltiness, how can it be made salty again? It is no longer good for anything, except to be thrown out and trampled underfoot. You are the light of the world. A town built on a hill cannot be hidden. Neither do people light a lamp and put it under a bowl. Instead they put it on its stand, and it gives light to everyone in the house. In the same way, let your light shine before others, that they may see your good deeds and glorify your Father in heaven* (Matthew 5:13-16).

» *I solemnly urge you in the presence of God and Christ Jesus, who will someday judge the living and the dead when He appears to set up His Kingdom: Preach the word of God. Be prepared, whether the time is favorable or not. Patiently correct, rebuke, and encourage your people with good teaching. For a time is coming when people will no longer listen to sound and wholesome teaching. They will follow their own desires and will look for teachers who will tell them whatever their itching ears want to hear. They will reject the truth and chase after myths. But you should keep a clear mind in every situation. Don't be afraid of suffering for the Lord. Work at telling others the Good News, and fully carry out the ministry God has given you* (2 Timothy 4:1-5 NLT).

According to Wikipedia, about 31% of the world's population is Christian - 2.2 billion people! **That makes God's holy nation the largest nation on earth!** Look around you the next time you go to church. You are brothers and sisters with all those who are believers in Christ, both in your church and around the world. Collectively, we are the Body of Christ! Imagine if all 2.2 billion of us were actively working together with a common mission – His Mission – to be and make disciples who are salt and light in the world! That will happen if we stop allowing Satan to win through his "divide and conquer" strategy! As the old saying goes, "Many hands make light the work."

Christ prayed for this unity so we know it is His will and therefore, He will be "with us":

» *Sanctify them by the truth; Your word is truth. As You sent me into the world, I have sent them into the world. For them I sanctify Myself, that they too may be truly sanctified. My prayer is not for them alone.* ***I pray also for those who will believe in Me through their message, that all of them may be one,*** *Father, just as You are in Me and I am in You. May they also be in Us so that the world may believe that You have sent Me. I have given them the glory that You gave Me, that they may be one as We are One: I in them and You in Me –* ***so that they may be brought to complete unity. Then the world will know that You sent Me*** *and have loved them even as You have loved Me* (John 17:17-23).

Wouldn't you agree that it is about time for all 2.2 billion of us to work as one body, making disciples, teaching them in truth and love to obey everything Christ taught us?

Remember who you are – a child of Almighty God! Do not get discouraged. You can fulfill your calling! Christ has created you with special talents and He will equip you and empower you to fulfill your purpose. Do not let the enemy tell you different or derail you from your personal calling and spiritual growth!

» *Do not worry about what to say or how to say it. At that time you will be given what to say, for it will not be you speaking, but the Spirit of your Father speaking through you* (Matthew 10:19-20).

» *The Advocate, the Holy Spirit, whom the Father will send in My name, will teach you all things and will remind you of everything I have said to you* (John 14:26).

» *But you have an anointing from the Holy One, and all of you know the truth* (1 John 2:20).

» *As for you, the anointing you received from Him remains in you, and you do not need anyone to teach you. But as His anointing teaches you about all things and as that anointing is real, not counterfeit — just as it has taught you, remain in Him* (1 John 2:27).

Remember who we are – a holy nation working together to build the Kingdom of God on earth! Go wherever God calls you, at home or abroad. Go into the neighborhood, the marketplace, the government, the schools, the churches, the non-profits, etc. Be disciples. Be ambassadors. Be salt and light. Do good works in His Name as you go so the world can see the goodness of God the Father. Go with the confidence that if you follow Christ's teaching, He is *with you* and *in you.*

Stay connected to The Vine as you go so He is "with you."

» *Anyone who loves Me will obey My teaching. My Father will love them, and We will come to them and make Our home with them. Anyone who does not love Me will not obey My teaching. These words you hear are not My own; they belong to the Father Who sent Me. All this I have spoken while still with you. But the Advocate, the Holy Spirit, whom the Father will send in My name, will teach you all things and will remind you of everything I have said to you. Peace I leave with you; My peace I give you. I do not give to you as the world gives. Do not let your hearts be troubled and do not be afraid* (John 14:23-27).

» *I am the Vine; you are the branches. If you remain in Me and I in you, you will bear much fruit; apart from Me you can do nothing. If you do not remain in Me, you are like a branch that is thrown away and withers; such branches are picked up, thrown into the fire and burned.* ***If you remain in Me and My words remain in you, ask whatever you wish, and it will be done for you.*** *This is to My Father's*

> *glory, that you bear much fruit, showing yourselves to be My disciples* (John 15:5-8).

IT IS FINISHED!

Jesus Christ has already defeated Satan and his forces of darkness. *And having disarmed the powers and authorities, He made a public spectacle of them, triumphing over them by the cross* (Colossians 2:15). With this truth firmly embedded in you, you will walk in His power and His protection, not yours.

You can do this! How am I so sure? Because the Bible tells you that if you hold to His Teachings, it will not be you doing these things, it will be Christ living in you Who is doing them.

I have become its servant by the commission God gave me to present to you the word of God in its fullness— the mystery that has been kept hidden for ages and generations, but is now disclosed to the Lord's people. To them God has chosen to make known among the Gentiles the glorious riches of this mystery, which is Christ in you, the hope of glory. He is the one we proclaim, admonishing and teaching everyone with all wisdom, so that we may present everyone fully mature in Christ (Colossians 1:25-28).

"The Bible is the weapon which enables us to join with our Lord on the offensive in defeating the spiritual hosts of wickedness. But it must be the Bible as the Word of God in everything it teaches - in matters of salvation, but just as much where it speaks of history and science and morality. If we compromise in any of these areas... we destroy the power of the Word and ourselves in the hands of the enemy" (Francis A. Schaeffer, *The Great Evangelical Disaster*).

Don't forget to put on The **Full** Armor of God today - and every day – as you *Hold to His Teaching,* so you *Stand Firm With God's Power In Business.* Then you will *Walk in His Protection* and

Live in His Blessings!

IF YOU LOVE ME,

KEEP MY COMMANDS.

MY COMMAND IS THIS:
LOVE EACH OTHER AS I HAVE LOVED YOU.

ALL AUTHORITY IN HEAVEN AND ON EARTH
HAS BEEN GIVEN TO ME.
THEREFORE GO AND MAKE DISCIPLES
OF ALL NATIONS...
TEACHING THEM TO OBEY EVERYTHING
I HAVE COMMANDED YOU.

AND SURELY I AM WITH YOU ALWAYS,
TO THE VERY END OF THE AGE.

I WILL BUILD MY CHURCH;
AND THE GATES OF HADES SHALL NOT OVERPOWER IT.

Jesus Christ, King of the Kingdom of God

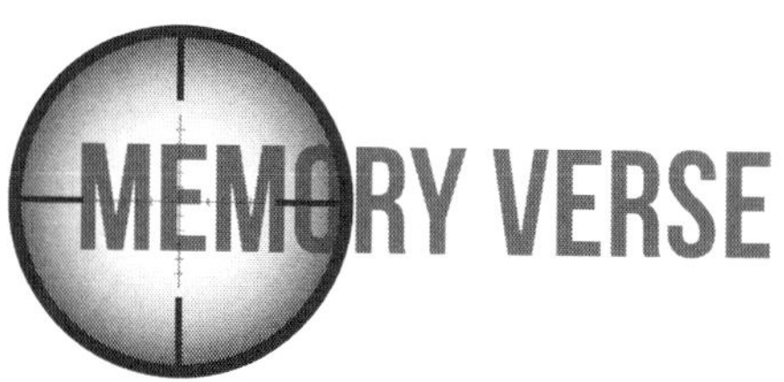

I have given them the glory that You gave Me, that they may be one as We are one - I in them and You in Me – so that they may be brought to complete unity. Then the world will know that You sent Me and have loved them even as You have loved Me.

John 17:22-23

QUESTIONS FOR CONSIDERATION:

- What is the Great Commission? How is it applicable to those of us who work in the marketplace?
- Why did Christ give it to those who believe in Him?
- Who is a disciple of Christ? Are you a disciple?
- Can someone be a Christian and not be a disciple?
- How is Christ calling you to help build His Kingdom?

BONUS CHAPTER

"It is as great and as difficult
a spiritual calling
to run the factories
and the mines,
the banks
and the department stores,
the schools
and government agencies
for the Kingdom of God
as it is to pastor a church
or serve as an evangelist."

Dallas Willard

that move along the ground (Genesis 1:26). *The Lord God took the man and put him in the Garden of Eden to work it and take care of it* (Genesis 2:15). Work is not the consequence of Adam and Eve's disobedience. The consequence of their disobedience is intolerable work – unproductive painful labor. *Cursed is the ground because of you; through painful toil you will eat food from it all the days of your life. It will produce thorns and thistles for you, and you will eat the plants of the field* (Genesis 3:17-18). God's original plan was that mankind would work, creatively develop the earth and populate it.

The organizational structures and business wisdom discussed throughout Scripture demonstrates that commerce and business were part of God's original design.

The LORD demands accurate scales and balances; He sets the standards for fairness (Proverbs 16:11 NLT).

Do your planning and prepare your fields before building your house (Proverbs 24:27 NLT).

Good comes to those who lend money generously and conduct their business fairly (Psalms 112:5 NLT).

Now listen, you who say, "Today or tomorrow we will go to this or that city, spend a year there, carry on business and make money." Why, you do not even know what will happen tomorrow. What is your life? You are a mist that appears for a little while and then vanishes. Instead, you ought to say, "If it is the Lord's will, we will live and do this or that." As it is, you boast in your arrogant schemes. All such boasting is evil (James 4:13-16).

There are sound reasons why many business owners believe that God has called them into business. There's the obvious need to provide a livelihood for other people. There's the dominion mandate to "be fruitful and multiply." There's the fact that we only live one life and we want to do all we can for God. But Baer says that, "In much of the world there is a fundamental conviction among sincere Christians that there is something intrinsically wrong with business and no serious follower of Christ would go into business, much less consider it a calling." In reality, the "goodness" of a business is dependent on the people running the business, just like any other organization.

Amazingly, there are Christian business owners who believe you absolutely cannot mix Christianity and business. This is obviously an erroneous belief because the Bible says clearly that God can play a significant role in the success or failure of the business: *You may say to yourself, 'My power and the strength of my hands have produced this wealth for me.' But remember the LORD your God, for it is He who gives you the ability to produce wealth, and so confirms His covenant* (Deuteronomy 8:17-18a).

It is no wonder that erroneous beliefs such as these have penetrated Christianity, when you consider that Satan - who is constantly at war with Christians - is referred to by the Lord Jesus Christ as *a liar and the father of lies* (John 8:44). Beliefs such as these are nothing more than lies, one of the core schemes of the devil to derail Christian business owners from assisting in successfully building the Kingdom of God. The whole of Scripture is that Christians are to be "in the world" but not "of the world." *My prayer is not that you take them out of the world but that you protect them from the evil one. They are not of the world, even as I am not of it* (John 17:15-16). This concept is part of your true identity as a child of God.

"There are two key ways Satan will try to destroy your business or make it ineffective"

I know of other business owners who avoid (knowingly or unknowingly) building a Kingdom business because they are not sure they want to struggle with"the world" and the increased spiritual warfare it will bring into their lives. Of course, their concerns are well founded. However, as discussed in this book, we do not need to be intimidated by the enemy – *You, dear children, are from God and have overcome them, because the One Who is in you is greater than the one who is in the world* (1 John 4:4). Nor by people he sends to discourage us - *For our struggle is not against flesh and blood, but against the rulers, against the authorities, against the powers of this dark world and against the spiritual forces of evil in the heavenly realms* (Ephesians 6:12).

Once, during the fledgling days of building American Business Advisors® (ABA), our Director of Marketing consultant walked up to me and said, "Benson, you are a dangerous person to work for!" "What are you talking about?" I asked. He was well familiar with spiritual warfare. "Before I came to work for you, my life was running smoothly. Now Satan is attacking me on every front!" he answered.

Why was he experiencing this? Because ABA was founded with a Kingdom business objective - assisting small and mid-sized Christian business owners with increasing profits and advancing through the phases of business growth in order to help fund the Great Commission and build the Kingdom of God. Although we also work with non-Christian business owners, this objective seemed to be a major threat to Satan.

"I know the plans I have for you," declares the LORD, "plans to prosper you and not to harm you, plans to give you hope and a future."

Jeremiah 29:11

Fear is a powerful core strategy of Satan to try to stop the advance of Christ's Church on earth. At times during the growth and development of ABA - and other companies I co-founded - I felt like Public Enemy #1 of the forces of darkness. Frankly, I always wondered why the enemy was so focused on a guy from a small town in Nebraska, like me. But as the late Dr. Vernon Grounds once told me, "God is the great chess player." Now in the hands of a great chess player, nothing is unintentional – every move has a purpose. Perhaps Satan knew I would write this book someday. Only he and God know. Nevertheless, because of God's wisdom and supernatural help, Christian business owners that ABA served over the years have given millions of dollars to Kingdom causes and some have become intentional about building the Kingdom on earth.

As Christian business leaders, we can't allow the enemy to persuade us that he is more powerful than Christ our King! Consider the following Scriptures while facing your fears:

» *I will build my church, and the gates of Hades* ***will not*** *overcome it* (Matthew 16:18).

» *Be strong and courageous. Do not be afraid; do not be discouraged, for the Lord your God will be* ***with you*** *wherever you go"* (Joshua 1:9).

KINGDOM BUSINESS DEFINED

You may be wondering, what is a "Kingdom Business"? What does Bob mean by that?" Good question. Most Christian businessmen I have known over the years think of their business as a Christian business. Meaning, they try to run it according to Biblical principles in such a way as to bring glory to God. Some even work God into their mission statement.

To answer the question, let's define a **secular business** first – a business owned by non-Christians whose mission is to provide a quality product or service to their marketplace. In the process, they may or may not use principles that are consistent with the Bible. Many sound business principles originally came from the Bible and are integrated into the world's business systems and beliefs (the world may not acknowledge that this is so – but it is)! Some of these principles include concepts such as: servant leadership, compounding wealth, multiplication, effective organizational structures, sound money management, kindness in dealing with people, integrity, etc. Secular businesses are not using them because they came from the Bible; they use them because they work! They work because God crafted the tangible world, people and natural laws to function and perform better when using His ways.

A **Christian business** may be indistinguishable by most from a secular business on the outside. It may have a similar mission of providing a quality product or service to the market and backing it up with exceptional customer service. It purposely uses Biblical principles in its values and operation, and since it is owned by a Christian, it is likely that the owner recognizes many of these principles in God's Word. To most of the world, its only noticeable difference is that it is owned and/or run by a Christian.

A **Kingdom business**, similar to a Christian business, is owned by a Believer who also uses Biblical principles and values, but its mission is specifically and intentionally focused on the establishment of the Kingdom of Christ on earth. This does not mean that the company avoids profit – profit is a good and holy thing in Scripture. According to The Promise, God gives believers wealth to be a blessing to "all peoples on earth": *I will make you into a great nation and I will bless you; I will make your name great, and you will be a blessing… all peoples on earth will be blessed through you* (Genesis 12:2-3). Remember, the believers in Christ are part of that "great nation." See chapter 3. Building a Kingdom Business just means that the owner's primary objective is assisting King Jesus with His Mission.

BUSINESS IS A HIGH CALLING FROM GOD

If you felt intentionally led to start your business, it could be that your business is the mission field that God has called you to. If you believe you have such a leadership calling from God, you are likely correct. Though you are faced with a challenging job, do not let your hearts be troubled. God has created you with that objective in mind: *For You created my inmost being; You knit me together in my mother's womb. I praise You because I am fearfully and wonderfully made; Your works are wonderful, I know that full well. My frame was not hidden from You when I was made in the secret place. When I was woven together in the depths of the earth, Your eyes saw my unformed body. All the days ordained for me were written in Your book before one of them came to be* (Psalm 139:13-16).

Some Christian leaders imply that Christians lead three separate lives, and that they are prioritized in this order: spiritual, family and business. This does not agree with the Bible. Scripture teaches us that we have one life and we are to live it for our Lord Jesus Christ in the building of his Kingdom. *Whatever you do, work at it with all your heart, as working for the Lord, not for human masters, since you know that you will receive an inheritance from the Lord as a reward. It is the Lord Christ you are serving* (Colossians 3:23-24).

The renowned author, Os Guinness, in his book *The Call – Finding and Fulfilling the Central Purpose of Your Life,* defines the notion of calling this way: "Calling is the truth that God calls us to Himself so decisively that everything we are, everything we do, and everything we have is invested with a special devotion, dynamism, and direction lived out as a response to His summons and service."

"A Kingdom Business is intentionally connected to the establishment of Christ's Kingdom in this world."
– Michael Baer

FINDING YOUR KINGDOM PURPOSE

Baer, a businessman and former pastor, points out that God the Father "is a God of purpose and plans, that He has an end in mind for the things he does and creates." The Bible teaches us that we each have a purpose. *In Him we were also chosen, having been predestined according to the plan of Him who works out everything in conformity with the purpose of His will* (Ephesians 1:11). *For we are God's handiwork, created in Christ Jesus to do good works, which God prepared in advance for us to do* (Ephesians 2:10).

I will build My church – Christ

God has a plan to build the Church, the Body of Christ, and

in so doing, to redeem all of creation. *The creation waits in eager expectation for the sons of God to be revealed. For the creation was subjected to frustration, not by its own choice, but by the will of the One who subjected it, in hope that the creation itself will be liberated from its bondage to decay and brought into the glorious freedom of the children of God* (Romans 8:19-21).

If God has rescued your life by calling you to become His child, He has called you into the Kingdom of God in some fashion. As such, *If you belong to Christ, then you are Abraham's seed, and heirs according to the promise* (Galatians 3:29). If you are a business owner, and He has called you into the Kingdom of God, then it is likely He has called you into business to assist the Lord Jesus Christ, in some fashion, with His plan. And if you obey His teaching, He is with you as you build your business. God's specifics in integrating your purpose with His are different for each person and therefore you must ask and seek Him to know those specifics for your life (Romans 12:1-2).

INTENTIONALITY

Baer says "a Kingdom business is intentional." It involves intentionally integrating your God-given purpose with God's purposes in the Bible. *For there is one body and one Spirit, just as you have been called to one glorious hope for the future. There is one Lord, one faith, one baptism, and one God and Father, who is over all and in all and living through all. However, He has given each one of us a special gift through the generosity of Christ* (Ephesians 4:4-7 NLT).

Be intentional and strategic about your decisions, knowing that God will direct your steps. *Trust in the LORD with all your heart; do not depend on your own understanding. Seek His will in all you do, and He will show you which path to take* (Proverbs 3:5-6 NLT).

Ask Him for help in building your Kingdom business with absolute confidence that, if you *Stand Firm With God's Power*, He will be with you and will help you because building the Kingdom of God is according to His will. *This is the confidence we have in approaching God: that if we ask anything according to His will, He hears us. And if we know that He hears us - whatever we ask - we know that we have what we asked of Him* (1 John 5:14-15).

EQUIPPING YOURSELF FOR THE JOB

If you are planning to build and lead a Kingdom business, Satan is going to use his arsenal of schemes against you, centering around two core strategic imperatives: 1) Exploiting areas where you are spiritually immature; and 2) Exploiting areas where you are immature in sound business practices. Therefore, you are going to need knowledge and understanding of sound business practices and how to use them. And you will need to know how to use Kingdom resources, as explained in this book, so you are equipped for all three struggles affecting your spiritual growth. These are the struggles with 1) the world, 2) the flesh, and 3) the devil. The last two have been covered in this book. I would like to add a few thoughts about our struggle with the "world."

> You may say to yourself, 'My power and the strength of my hands have produced this wealth for me.' But remember the LORD your God, for it is He who gives you the ability to produce wealth, and so confirms His covenant.
>
> Deuteronomy 8:17-18a

The battle with "the world" requires an understanding of Satan's system of behavior and lies. Primarily, they are the opposite of God's system of behavior and truth. The primary issue in business is to know Kingdom economic and people principles well enough to recognize the difference between them and Satan's principles that are integrated into "the world."

For a good study of God's core Kingdom economic principles, I recommend you read the book, *Secrets of the Kingdom Economy,* by Paul Cuny. Paul has been a businessman his whole life and speaks internationally on the topic.

God's people principles are simple: *Love your neighbor as yourself* (Mark 12:31) and *Do to others as you would have them do to you* (Luke 6:31). There are many good Christian books on how to manage people, including *Lead like Jesus* by Ken Blanchard and Phil Hodges and *Leading the Followers by Following the Leader* by Dennis L. Gorton.

FACING DOWN THE PRINCIPLES OF THE WORLD

In January 2005, I was introduced to a client by a banker because we "shared the same values." He and his wife were Christians. I will call their business Company A. They had been in business for seven years and were just finishing a year with $9.7 million in sales and a $25,000 net profit before taxes. After seven years in business they had only accumulated $268,000 in equity, but they had accumulated about $2.1 million in debt, including a $1 million line of credit (LOC). This represented a 7.8:1 debt to equity ratio. Not enough equity to run a thriving business in any economic system.

They believed the business could do $15 million in business in 2005 and they needed to increase the LOC to accommodate the expected growth. The bank was not interested in the loan because the company was under-capitalized and under-performing. There were many reasons for the lack of profits and equity, one of which was $61,000 in donations to Christian organizations, which were made on the company books.

We began working on their financial forecast and reengineering their strategies for 2005 to improve their competitive position and develop a sound pricing, cost and margin structure. After I earned their trust, I confronted them on the amount of money they were giving away to Christian organizations (the sacred cow for these owners) representing 71% of their profits. I took my Bible out of the briefcase and read Deuteronomy 28 to them, explaining that what they were doing with debt and giving was not Biblical. I explained that, according to Scripture, God wants to bless us to the point that we have little or no debt so we can be a "blessing to all nations." I went on to explain that reducing debt can't happen if they give away most of the surplus God provides for them, instead of tithing as God has requested. *You will lend to many nations but will borrow from none,* God declares in Deuteronomy 28:12.

God also tells us in Malachi Chapter 3, that we are stealing from Him if we do not tithe. You will hear many differing opinions on this topic. If they do not line up with the teaching about tithing in Scripture, do not listen to them. Our Father and His Son control everything that goes on in the universe! Is it really worth the risk? Personally, I have found you cannot out-give God.

Since I am both an entrepreneur and a CPA, I deeply understand there is a time and need for debt. But it should not be so much debt that it threatens the sustainability and peak performance of your company. Once profitability is established, wise Christian business owners in most industries manage their debt down to between a .4:1 and 1:1 debt-to-equity ratio. I have run numbers on hundreds of companies and most industries. The fact is that the top 25% financial performing businesses in the vast majority of the industries have a debt-to-equity ratio of less than one to one (1:1). The mismanagement of surplus in businesses owned by Christians is one of Satan's grand strategies to steal from them, keep them weak and unable to thrive.

Back to the story: I went on to recommend to Company A to not give any more money away until the end of the year so we could build equity and obtain the LOC we needed. I promised them that if they followed these recommendations, based on Kingdom principles, they would be able to give a lot more money away at year end, even give "offerings" in addition to a tithe. After preparing their business plan and financial forecast, integrating the strategies and tactics we developed together, I recommended we target $13 million in sales instead of $15 million because that was the number that would maximize their profits and equity, allowing the business to thrive and obtain a larger LOC at cheaper interest rates. We forecasted $999,000 in net income before income taxes.

During the year, as we proved out the plan, a new bank gave them a $1.2 million LOC, at a considerably lower interest rate, to facilitate the growth. Company A did $12 million in business that year and made $720,000 in net income before income taxes (270% more profit than they had made cumulative since they started the business). And the owners personally gave away about $120,000 in donations out of the profits. At the end of the year their debt-to-equity ratio was 2.1:1, an acceptable ratio to the banking community.

In spite of the fact that the company needed the capital to grow and thrive, most of Company A's advisors instructed the owners to spend money at year end and take money out to minimize income taxes. I advised the opposite. The bank told them after the next year end of profitability that they would increase their LOC again and offered to finance a building for them.

FURTHER ACTION STEPS TO GUIDE YOU IN BUILDING A KINGDOM BUSINESS

The call to build a Kingdom business is truly a holy calling! If you believe that God is leading you to this endeavor, here are some additional recommended action steps to guide you in building the Kingdom business that the Lord has anointed you for:

» Follow the Spiritual Action Plan you developed in Chapter 9. If you don't, Satan will make your life miserable!

» In addition to the books above, *Read Business as Mission* by Michael R. Baer. This is a MUST READ and it has some very sound advice for determining your business' Kingdom purposes, managing relationships, developing excellence, planning for establishing a Kingdom Business and more.

» Ask Christ for protection and the ability to produce wealth to do good works with. Remember, if you are building it His way, it is He who gives you the ability to produce wealth (Deuteronomy 8:18).

» Read books, take business courses or seminars, hire executive level managers as you can afford them, utilize professional advisors and hire a qualified business coach/ consultant to instruct you in sound business practices throughout your business growth. You will experience higher profits and faster growth.

» Ask Christ for wisdom, knowledge and understanding about how to build a business His way, so that you *may have the full riches of complete understanding, in order that they may know the mystery of God, namely, Christ, in whom are hidden all the treasures of wisdom and knowledge* (Colossians 2:2-3). This is the most important because, through the Holy Spirit, He will lead you to all the truth you need and will counsel you on how to use the knowledge and put together the pieces of the jigsaw puzzle to build your business.

- Obey God! All these blessings will come on you and accompany you if you obey the LORD your God (Deuteronomy 28:2).
- Pray about everything!

And of course, don't forget to put on The **Full** Armor of God today - and every day. As you *Hold to His Teaching,* He will enable you to stand firm with His Power in business. Then you will *Walk in His Protection* and *Live in His Blessings!*

WHEN YOU EAT AND ARE SATISFIED,

WHEN YOU BUILD FINE HOUSES

AND SETTLE DOWN

AND WHEN YOUR HERDS AND FLOCKS GROW LARGE

AND YOUR SILVER AND GOLD INCREASE

AND ALL YOU HAVE IS MULTIPLIED

YOU MAY SAY TO YOURSELF,

"MY POWER AND THE STRENGTH OF MY HANDS

HAVE PRODUCED THIS WEALTH FOR ME."

BUT REMEMBER THE LORD YOUR GOD,

FOR IT IS HE WHO GIVES YOU THE ABILITY

TO PRODUCE WEALTH,

AND SO CONFIRMS HIS COVENANT.

Moses

Remember the LORD your God, for it is He who gives you the ability to produce wealth, and so confirms His covenant...

Deuteronomy 8:17-18

QUESTIONS FOR CONSIDERATION:

- What is a Kingdom Business? What is the difference between a Christian business and a Kingdom business?
- Why are you in business?
- Do you see your business as a calling from God?
- What legacy do you want to leave when you die?
- What is Christ calling you to do with your business?

EPILOGUE

If *my* people,
who are called by
My name,
will humble themselves
and pray
and seek *My* face
and turn from
their wicked ways,
then I will hear
from Heaven
and will forgive
their sins
and will heal
their land.

2 Chronicles 7:13-15

EPILOGUE

What do you want for your life? - Your family? - Your career? - Your business? If you are like every person I have ever talked to around the world, you want the best. So does your Father. You want unity. So does your Father. You want to be you. Your Father created you to be you. You want to be free from the baggage of weaknesses and addictions. Your Father wants to see you free. You want to be successful. Your Father wants to give you the desires of your heart! You want to be a blessing to others. Your Father has blessed you to be a blessing. You want to live in peace. Your Father sent you the Prince of Peace. You want to live in a safe nation. Your Father turns the hearts of kings. You want to be loved and appreciated. Your Father loves you and wants others to love you.

In this book, I have shared some of my weaknesses and my successes with you. But like the Apostle Paul, I prefer to brag about my weaknesses, because in that part of my story lays the secret to your winning strategies in life and your battle with the enemy and his forces of darkness. *I will not boast about myself, except about my weaknesses. Three times I pleaded with the Lord to take it away from me. But he said to me, "My grace is sufficient for you, for My power is made perfect in weakness." Therefore I will boast all the more gladly about my weaknesses, so that Christ's power may rest on me. That is why, for Christ's sake, I delight in weaknesses, in insults, in hardships, in persecutions, in difficulties. For when I am weak, then I am strong* (2 Corinthians 12:5,8-10).

I shared with you that in the early 80's, I was a Christian, but I was not fully obeying God in my life. Although I didn't recognize it at the time, I was taking credit for my own success. I believed that God gives each of us special gifts which enable our success, but I was ignorant of the enormous extent of God's involvement in my life. To teach me this, God dialed down my gift for a while – creating difficulty, burdens, toil and a decline in my success.

A company hired me to turn their business around. I felt impotent, unproductive and as though the customer was being cheated. Not that I was slacking – I was working eight to ten hours a day, but I knew I wasn't at my best – that is, the best I could be when God was "with me." After five or six months, a few top level company executives came into my office. I thought, "Oh boy. They are disappointed with my work." Instead, they thanked and praised me, saying, "You are really doing a good job and making a big difference around here. We appreciate all that you do." After they left, I scratched my head and asked God what was going on. God responded, "It's not you, it's Me doing these things."

Around that time, I had read a story on the life of D.L. Moody. One day, Moody was walking down the street and he suddenly felt overwhelmed by an anointing of God so strong that he had to walk in off the street and check into a hotel. He later reported that after that experience with the Lord he didn't really do anything different, but his messages seemed to have more power and the effectiveness of his ministry greatly increased.

You see, when God gives you a spiritual gift, He is not only anointing you, He anoints and works in the lives of the whole environment around you. Later in life, I realized that when I got out of college God suddenly gave me the spiritual gift of administration (or some Bible versions say "leadership"). But while going through life, I gradually took the credit for it. Combined with little or no knowledge of Satan's schemes and his involvement in my decision-making on a day-to-day basis, I was easy prey for him.

Such is the work of Satan and his forces of evil. And so it is in the world today. 76% of the population of the U.S. are taking the name of Christ by calling themselves a "Christian."

Millions of those Christians engage in almost daily conversations about the declining condition of the U.S. and the values of its population. They blame the governments and non-Christians for this condition. Blaming others – another one of Satan's schemes! But the Bible says that "our battle is not against flesh and blood."

What then is God's solution for a nation's declining spiritual condition? *If My people, who are called by My name, will humble themselves and pray and seek My face and turn from their wicked ways, then will I hear from Heaven and will forgive their sin and will heal their land* (2 Chronicles 7:13-15).

Once I made the choice to take 100% responsibility for my behavior and change it, I set my mind on "what the Spirit desires" and He has led me to the truth I needed. Then He counseled me, directly and indirectly through others, leading me safely through the process of sanctification. He taught me how to get out from under the control of the *old nature* and live under the control of the *new nature.*

This has taken several years and the daily maintenance continues to this day. But as a result, I more fully obey God and as He promised, He *restored my soul* and He has been *with me* once again. He has showed me how to overcome Satan through Him, by putting on His armor. Again I say, "If I can do it, anyone can." But wait, the whole point of this book is to teach you that you can't do it. It wasn't me doing these things, it was Christ in me. He will do the same for you if you ask Him. That's why anyone can do it!

He will heal our land if Christians, calling themselves by His name and citizens of His Nation, will pray, seek His face, turn from their wicked ways, and do life (and business) His way. Then, He will be with them and heal their land.

ABOUT THE AUTHOR

ABOUT THE AUTHOR

Robert C. Benson III (Bob) is a layperson with no seminary degree. He writes articles for The Spirit Led Business™ newsletter, with an objective of providing practical applications for laypeople in business to apply Scripture in their day-to-day lives. This book is written with that objective in mind.

Bob is co-founder and president of American Business Advisors, Inc (ABA), a strategic and management consulting firm specializing in the development of small and mid-sized companies through the phases of business growth. He is a Certified Management Consultant (CMC) and a Certified Public Accountant (CPA*). Bob has been a business advisor to hundreds of companies and is also an accomplished entrepreneur, founding or co-founding seven businesses. Before co-founding ABA in 1984 he was founder and the Managing Partner of Benson Wells & Co., CPA's (now Corne Jantz & Associates P.C.); and co-founder and past president of SecurCare Self Storage, Inc., one of the ten largest self-storage companies in America.

Mr. Benson has a B.A. degree from Dakota Wesleyan University with majors in Business Administration and Mathematics and a Minor in Economics. He has also taken additional course studies in marketing and finance from the University of Colorado, Denver, and numerous continuing education courses offered by the CPA profession and others since 1970. His other professional accomplishments and associations include: Member of the Institute of Management Consultants, American Institute of Certified Public Accountants and Colorado Society of Certified Public Accountants;

Past member of the Professional Practice Board and past Vice Chairman of the Accounting and Auditing Procedures Committee of the Colorado Society of CPA's; Lecturer, Center for Leadership Development, Kiev, Ukraine; Author of numerous business articles; Publisher/Editor of The Strategic Edge™ business newsletter; and Publisher/Editor of The Spirit Led Business™ newsletter.

Over the period beginning in 1970, Bob has also been active in various non-profits, as a board member of Child Evangelism (St. Paul, MN), Christian Business Men's Committee (St. Paul, MN), Denver Youth for Christ, Southern Gables Evangelical Church, Cherry Hills Community Church, COMPA Food Ministry, Project C.U.R.E. and Global Connections International.

Currently Bob is President of The Colorado Christian Business Alliance and serves on its board and the boards of Dakota Wesleyan University and Love & Logic Institute.

Born in 1944 in Waukegan, Illinois while Bob's father was an officer and drill instructor in the U.S. Navy, he grew up in Bancroft and Lyons, small towns in Eastern Nebraska. Bob is married to Ree Ann, his junior high sweetheart. They have been married since 1961 and have two sons and four grandchildren.

Since 1973, Bob has devoted a significant amount of his time to studying Scripture, with an emphasis on understanding living in the "new nature" and spiritual warfare, including its effect on him, his family, his business and the Body of Christ in general. He is passionate about declaring God's faithfulness and discipling Christians concerning Kingdom economics and spiritual warfare.

Bob Benson can be contacted at bob@ABAdvisors.com

Paperback and Kindle books can be purchased at amazon.com

7419910R00140

Made in the USA
San Bernardino, CA
07 January 2014